INDIAN CHIEFS

A Sioux Chief. From a drawing by Frederic Remington.

INDIAN CHIEFS

RUSSELL FREEDMAN

Holiday House / New York

Library of Congress Cataloging-in-Publication Data

Freedman, Russell.
Indian chiefs.

SUMMARY: Biographies of six Western Indian chiefs
who led their people in a historic moment of crisis,
when a decision had to be made about fighting or
cooperating with the white pioneers encroaching on
their hunting grounds.
1. Indians of North America—Biography—Juvenile
literature.   [1. Indians of North America—Biography]
I. Title.
E89.F73   1987   970.004′ 97   [920]   86-46198
ISBN 0-8234-0625-3
ISBN 0-8234-0971-6 (pbk)

For George and Carol Hutchinson

CONTENTS

INDIAN CHIEFS

Sitting Bull, war chief and medicine man of the Hunkpapa Sioux. The eagle feathers on his war bonnet signify acts of daring and courage in battle.

WAR CHIEFS
and
PEACE CHIEFS

When Sitting Bull became a Sioux chief in the 1860s, he composed a song to help celebrate the event. At his inauguration, he wore a flowing war bonnet of eagle feathers that spilled down his back and swept onto the ground, and he sang out in his booming voice:

> Ye tribes, behold me!
> The chiefs of old are gone.
> Myself, I shall take courage.

He was going to need plenty of courage, for his people faced a grave and growing threat. They were threatened with the loss of their hunting grounds, their livelihood, and their freedom. All over the West, Indian tribes were being pushed from their lands by white settlers and soldiers.

3

Only twenty years earlier, when Sitting Bull was a boy, most of the territory west of the Mississippi River still belonged to the Indians and the buffalo. Dozens of tribes and bands, each with its own language and customs, were scattered across the western plains and mountains. These tribes were as different from one another as the different nations of Europe. Like the Europeans of that era, the Indians formed alliances with their friends and made war on their enemies, fighting hard among themselves for territory, for plunder, and for the thrills and glory of combat.

White explorers, fur trappers, and traders had been filtering into the West since the early 1800s. At first, the Indians they met seemed friendly enough. Most tribes welcomed the whites into their villages and were willing to live at peace with them. It wasn't until white settlers claimed Indian land, and the army built forts to protect the settlers, that the real troubles began.

The policy of the United States government was to set aside reservations where the Indians would live apart from the whites. Government officials hoped that the wandering tribes would settle down on these reservations, exchange their bows and arrows for shovels and plows, and learn to support themselves like the white settlers, by farming and ranching.

Many whites believed that the destiny of the United States was to settle the entire continent from coast to coast. The Indians stood in the way of civilization and progress. Army General George Crook told a group of Indian leaders exactly what to expect. "The white men in the East are like birds," said Crook. "They are hatching out their eggs every year, and there is not room enough in the East and they must go elsewhere. And they come west, as you have seen them coming for the last few years. And they are still coming, and will come

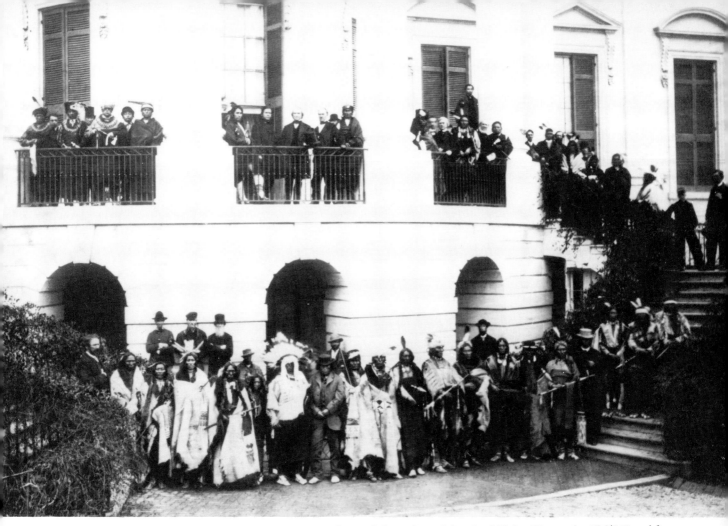

A Sioux delegation visits the White House in 1867. President Andrew Johnson stands in the center of the middle balcony, flanked by government officials and interpreters.

until they overrun all of this country. And you can't prevent it."

Some of the weaker tribes submitted to reservation life without a struggle. But most Indians did not take kindly to the government's plans for them. "The whites were always trying to make the Indians give up their way of life and live like the white men," said a Sioux chief. "If the Indians had tried to make the whites live like them, the whites would have resisted, and it was the same with many Indians."

Over the years, the Indians and whites met together at many councils and made many treaties. Boundary lines were marked off. Certain lands were assigned to the tribes to have and hold forever—or, as the treaties often said, "as long as waters run and the grass shall grow." Peace lasted a few years. But sooner or later, white hunters, miners, ranchers, and farmers would cross those boundary lines into Indian territory. The Indians would protest and strike back. After a period of warfare, a new treaty would be drawn up, and the Indians would sign away more of their territory.

Looking back at these events years later, an old Kiowa woman remarked: "The pieces of treaty paper on which the chiefs made their marks always said that we were to stop raiding, give up our captives, and stay on the reservation that the Great White Father was going to give us. It made no difference that the land he was giving us, and much more besides, was already ours and always had been. We soon began to notice that each time we made a treaty, we lost a little more land, although each time we were told that the new reservation was to be ours 'forever.' We never fully understood that by 'forever' the white man meant 'until we want it for ourselves.'"

As tensions increased, every Indian leader in the West had to choose a course of action. Should his people resist and make war? Or should they cooperate with the whites, try to save as much land as possible and at least part of their traditions? Many tribes chose to resist, but only the largest and most powerful were able to hold out for long against the United States Cavalry.

Often, the leaders of a tribe could not agree on what to do. The Kiowas, for example, were divided into two opposing groups—a peace faction that called for compromise with the whites, and a war faction that demanded all-out resistance.

6

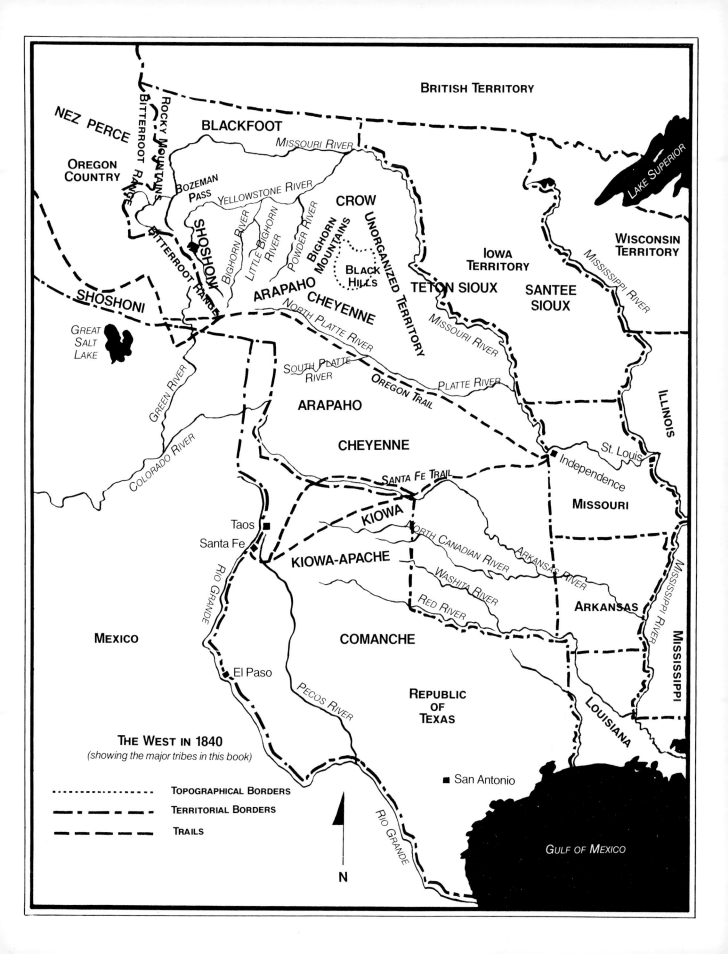

THE WEST IN 1840
(showing the major tribes in this book)

.... TOPOGRAPHICAL BORDERS
—··—··— TERRITORIAL BORDERS
— — — TRAILS

Warriors on the Nez Perce Reservation

The Kiowa chiefs spent long nights around their council fires debating their future course.

The whites usually applied the word *chief* to all Indian leaders, but Indian society wasn't that simple. Each tribe had many words in its language to distinguish among many levels and degrees of leadership. A small band might have several chiefs. The "war chiefs" were outstanding military leaders who organized raids and planned strategy during battles. "Peace chiefs" or "civil chiefs" supervised the daily life of the tribe, planning hunting expeditions, resolving disputes, and acting as spokesmen in meetings with other tribes and with the whites. Many tribes recognized one or more principal chiefs, but these men always shared their authority with other tribal leaders. A principal chief ranked as first among equals. He could advise but not command.

Some chiefs inherited their positions from their fathers, but in most cases, a chief had to earn his rank in the tribe. He

8

inspired loyalty and respect through his wisdom, his record of accomplishments, and the force of his personality. If people lost faith in him, then he was no longer their chief.

In the past, many inspiring leaders had appeared among the Indians of North America. The struggle between the Indians and the whites had been going on for more than two hundred years, since the first white colonists settled along the Atlantic coast. By the mid-1800s the eastern tribes had been defeated, subdued, and scattered, and the advancing frontier had caught up with the tribes that had always lived in the West. The six chiefs whose stories are told here were called upon to lead their people at a time of crisis. Each of these men tried to meet that challenge in his own way.

"Do not misunderstand me, but understand me fully with reference to my affection for the land," said Chief Joseph of the Nez Perce tribe. "I never said the land was mine to do with as I chose. The one who has the right to dispose of it is the one who has created it. I claim a right to live on my land, and accord you the privilege to live on yours."

Red Cloud

RED CLOUD

The Great Spirit raised me in this land,
and it belongs to me.

Painted and dressed for battle and singing war songs, the warriors formed orderly columns and rode out of their great encampment on the Powder River. They wore feathered war bonnets and buckskin shirts decorated with beads and porcupine quills, and they carried shields made of buffalo hide. Eagle feathers fluttered from the manes of their painted and prancing ponies. Red flannel banners and tassels of scarlet horsehair waved from every lance.

Leading the march were some celebrated war chiefs, among them Dull Knife of the Northern Cheyennes, Black Bear of the Arapahos, Hump of the Miniconjou Sioux, and Red Cloud of the Oglala Sioux. All together, some three thousand fighting men had joined the war party. On this July day in 1865 they were heading south to attack a U.S. Army garrison on the North Platte River, in the wilderness of the future state of Wyoming.

The valley of the Platte River had long been a busy overland highway for white emigrants traveling along the Oregon Trail.

North of the Platte, the remote Powder River country was still untamed Indian territory—the stronghold of the mighty Sioux and their allied tribes. Few whites had ventured into this region until 1862, when army engineers arrived to open a new road, the Bozeman Trail. The Indians regarded the Bozeman Trail as a threat to their hunting grounds. Angered by the intrusion, they had vowed to shut down the new road and keep the Powder River country free of whites.

"The Great Spirit raised me in this land, and it belongs to me," Red Cloud had said. "The white man was raised over the great waters, and his land is over there. Since they crossed the sea, I have given them room. There are now white people all about me. I have but a small spot of land left. The Great Spirit told me to keep it."

During the spring of 1865 Indian war parties had raided up and down the Platte Valley, ripping out telegraph wires and attacking wagon trains, coach stations, and army outposts. Now the Indians had organized a massive expedition. Red Cloud and his fellow war chiefs had decided to show their true strength and teach the white soldiers a lesson. They would strike at the point where the army troops were farthest north— the garrison on the North Platte River.

On July 24 the Indians reached the hills overlooking the river and the army post on the other side. At first, they tried to lure the soldiers into an ambush. But when the troopers realized that a huge war party was hiding in the sun-burnt hills, they refused to come out of their stockade.

The Indians waited. On the morning of July 26 an unsuspecting wagon train came rolling up the trail toward the fort. A platoon of cavalrymen galloped out of the stockade to warn the train and escort it to safety. The Indians swarmed down from the hills, overwhelmed both the troopers and the train,

On the Warpath. Lithograph by J. M. Stanley.

and after a wild fight, killed many of the whites.

Then the Indians withdrew. Satisfied with their victory, they returned to their villages up north. "If white men come into my country again," Red Cloud warned, "I will punish them again."

The origin of Red Cloud's name has always been a mystery. There are at least a dozen stories on the subject. According to one story, a meteorite roared over Sioux territory the night he was born, leaving a trail of red clouds behind it. Many Sioux babies born that winter were named Red Cloud.

Another story claims that Red Cloud as a boy had his grandfather's name, Two Arrows. When he was about nineteen years old, he led a Sioux war party in a battle against an enemy tribe. The Sioux warriors were wearing scarlet blankets over

13

their shoulders that day. As they swept down a hillside on their rushing ponies, they looked like an advancing red cloud, and the frightened enemy turned and fled. From then on, Two Arrows was known as Makh-pia-sha, or Red Cloud.

Red Cloud had been born during the winter of 1822 at a Sioux camp on the rolling prairie, near the present site of North Platte, Nebraska. His people were Oglalas, one of seven tribes belonging to the powerful Teton Sioux nation. His mother and father both died when he was a small boy. He was raised by his older sisters and a devoted uncle, White Hawk, who trained the youngster in the thousand skills of a Sioux hunter and warrior. White Hawk complained that his nephew was too wild and unruly. He often lectured the boy, saying that he had the makings of a great chief—if he could only rule his impulses.

Like every Sioux boy, Red Cloud began to track rabbits and other small game as soon as he was big enough to use the miniature bow and arrow his uncle had given him. As he grew older, he trained himself to run for hours without stopping, to go for days without food, to stay awake all night. He learned

A Sioux village on the Laramie River, 1874

to ride bareback, guiding his horse by the pressure of his knees and the shifting weight of his body. At a full gallop, he could scoop a pebble from the ground, leap from one horse to another, or hang over the side of his racing mount, holding on with elbows and knees as he used both hands to shoot a stream of arrows. By the time he was fifteen or sixteen, he was riding into battle with Oglala war parties, joining in raids and fights against the Crows and other enemies.

He proved his worth in battle many times, and he became famous for his good luck. Once, in a fight with some Pawnees, an arrow pierced his body from front to back, so that only the point and feathers were visible. These were broken off, and the shaft of the arrow was removed. Red Cloud recovered from the wound and quickly regained his strength.

He also became known as a doctor, or medicine man. During the summer of 1849 a cholera epidemic swept westward along the Oregon Trail, carried by emigrants bound for California and the Northwest. The disease spread quickly to the Indians, who had no natural immunity to diseases brought by the whites. The Sioux were convinced that they had been poisoned in some mysterious manner, but they were too sick and frightened to attempt reprisals. Red Cloud is said to have devised a remedy for cholera. He prepared an extract of cedar leaves, which was considered helpful to the sufferers.

By the early 1860s Red Cloud was recognized as a popular Oglala leader. Until then, the whites had paid little attention to the Indian country north of the Platte River. But all that changed in 1862 when gold was discovered in the mountains of present-day Montana. Within a year, miners and traders were pouring over the new Bozeman Trail, which branched off from the Oregon Trail near Fort Laramie and led north to the booming mining camps around Virginia City, Montana.

Peace council at Fort Laramie. U.S. government peace commissioners
met with Indian chiefs at Fort Laramie in 1866 and again in 1868.
The treaty signed here ended Red Cloud's War and established the
Great Sioux Reservation in what is now South Dakota.

The Bozeman Trail was an invitation to trouble. It cut
through the heart of the Powder River country, the prized
hunting grounds of the Sioux. They knew that other hunting
grounds had been ruined when the white men built roads
through them, and they promised each other that this would
not happen to them. Under Red Cloud's militant leadership,
Indian war parties began to strike at every wagon and pack
train that dared travel over the disputed trail. Soon the whites
were calling it "the Bloody Bozeman."

The road became so dangerous that in June 1866 the U.S.

government asked Red Cloud and other leading chiefs to attend a peace council at Fort Laramie. The chiefs agreed to talk. It seemed at first that they might be willing to end their attacks, if the government guaranteed that travelers on the Bozeman Trail would not disturb the game.

As the two sides negotiated, an army regiment commanded by Colonel Henry Carrington pulled into Fort Laramie. Carrington caused an uproar at the peace council when he revealed that he had been ordered to build a chain of forts along the Bozeman Trail. None of the chiefs had been told anything about the army's plan. One after another, they rose to denounce the army and accuse the peace commissioners of deceiving them.

Red Cloud was visibly angry when he took his turn at the speaker's platform. He stood there glaring—a tall, angular, hawk-faced man with piercing eyes and jet-black hair draped over his shoulders and hanging almost to his waist. The commissioners had treated the chiefs like children, he said. They had only been pretending to negotiate, while planning all along to take the Powder River country by force.

"The white men have crowded the Indians back year by year, until we are forced to live in a small country north of the Platte," Red Cloud continued. "Now our last hunting ground is to be taken from us. Our women and children will starve, but for my part, I prefer to die by fighting rather than starvation.... The Great Father [the President] sends us presents and wants us to sell him the road. But before the Indians can say yes or no, the white chief [Carrington] comes with his soldiers to steal the road."

While an interpreter was still translating his words into English, Red Cloud stormed out of the meeting, taking many of the other chiefs with him. The next day, they left Fort Laramie.

The chiefs who had stayed behind continued to negotiate. They signed a treaty agreeing to let white travelers use the Bozeman Trail. As Colonel Carrington moved north with his troops to build three forts on the road, Red Cloud sent word that he was ready to fight.

In the months that followed, Red Cloud and his allies carried on a hit-and-run guerrilla war, striking at wagon trains and military convoys all along the Bloody Bozeman, and raiding Colonel Carrington's garrisons at Forts Reno, Phil Kearny, and C. F. Smith. From every part of the Powder River country, Cheyenne, Arapaho, and Sioux warriors rode into Red Cloud's camp to join the battle. By late autumn, he had assembled four thousand fighting men.

Much of the fighting centered around Fort Kearny, which stood at the very heart of the Indians' hunting grounds. Red Cloud was certain he could win a decisive victory if he could somehow lure a large force of soldiers out of the fort. He began to plan an ambush.

His chance came on the morning of December 21, 1866 when a logging detail left Fort Kearny to collect firewood

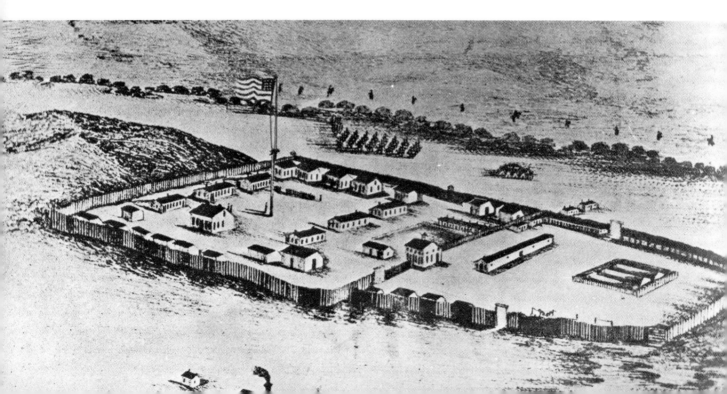

Captain William Fetterman led eighty cavalry troopers to a disastrous defeat on December 21, 1866.

along Big Piney Creek. About an hour later, at 11:00 A.M., an army lookout on a hill near the fort signaled with a flag that the loggers had been attacked.

Inside the fort, bugles sounded the alarm. A relief force was mustered and placed under the command of Captain William Fetterman, a young cavalry officer who had often expressed contempt for the Indians' fighting abilities. "Give me eighty men," Fetterman had boasted, "and I'll ride through the whole Sioux nation." As fate would have it, Fetterman was in charge of exactly eighty men when he rode out to rescue the beleaguered loggers.

Fetterman and his troopers were approaching when the Indians suddenly called off their attack and withdrew. The logging party started racing back to the fort and safety. A short time later, a few warriors were spotted close to the fort itself. They were moving slowly along the edge of the brush, some on horseback, others on foot, trying to stay out of sight. Two howitzer shells exploded over their heads, knocking one warrior off his horse. The other Indians howled and scattered.

19

Fort Phil Kearny. Built by Colonel Henry Carrington in 1866, evacuated and abandoned by the United States in 1868, the fort was immediately burned to the ground by Red Cloud's triumphant warriors. More battles and skirmishes were fought in the vicinity of this post than around any other fort on the western frontier.

Fetterman saw the fleeing warriors and decided to go after them.

The warriors were decoys, and they had carefully rehearsed the role they were about to play. There were ten of them—two Cheyennes, two Arapahos, and six Sioux. They were led by a young Sioux named Crazy Horse, who had a streak of lightning painted on his cheeks and the feathered skin of a hawk pinned to his hair.

The decoys moved back slowly, taunting the soldiers, shouting insults and threats, charging at them now and then as if to drive them back, then dashing away. Staying just beyond the range of the soldiers' rifles, they led the troopers into the hills, across Big Piney Creek, and up onto Lodge Trail Ridge.

Fetterman had been ordered not to chase the Indians past the ridge. But there were only ten of them against his eighty well-armed men, and he couldn't resist. As the decoys topped the ridge and galloped down onto the Bozeman Trail on the other side, Fetterman's strung-out relief force raced after them. The fort was now out of sight. Suddenly the decoys split into two groups, then veered and rode quickly across each other's trails. That was the signal for the ambush.

Some two thousand warriors had been waiting for the decoys to lead the soldiers into a trap. Whooping and yelling, they sprang from their hiding places in high grass and behind rocks and swarmed down on the startled troopers from every direction, showering them with arrows, swinging their hatchets and war clubs. Only a few of the Indians carried guns, but it hardly mattered. The soldiers were surrounded and overwhelmed as they tried to defend themselves with their rifles and bayonets.

The battle lasted about forty-five minutes. When it was over, Captain Fetterman and every one of his eighty men lay dead

A Sharp Encounter. Charles Schreyvogel's painting portrays a typical skirmish between mounted cavalrymen and Indian warriors.

on the field, stripped of their clothing, their weapons, and their scalps. It was the worst defeat the army had ever suffered in Indian warfare, and the first battle in U.S. history without a single American survivor. The Indians called it the Battle of the Hundred Slain. The whites began to call it the Fetterman Massacre.

The army rushed reinforcements into the Powder River country, and the war, now known as Red Cloud's War, continued. Red Cloud's forces kept the three forts on the Bozeman Trail in a constant state of siege. Soldiers manning the forts had to fight just to get food and water. Any white man who ventured onto the trail was risking his life. As the Indians kept up the pressure month after month, it became clear that the government must either make peace or face a long and costly conflict.

Once again, a peace commission traveled to Fort Laramie. A new treaty was drawn up that promised to grant the Indians' demands. Lavish gifts, including guns and ammunition, were offered to every chief who agreed to sign. The government planned to set aside all of present-day South Dakota west of the Missouri River as a reservation for the Sioux and their allies. The Powder River country, to the west of the reservation, would be declared "unceded Indian territory." This meant that the region would be off-limits to whites. It would be guaranteed as an Indian sanctuary forever, a place where the Sioux and their allies could roam and hunt at will.

In April 1868 the government's peace commissioners persuaded a number of important chiefs to come down to Fort Laramie and sign the new treaty. Red Cloud refused. He would not sign anything, he said, until the last soldier had left the Powder River country. He did send a message to the commissioners: "We are in the mountains looking down on the soldiers and the forts. When we see the soldiers moving away and the forts abandoned, then I will come down and talk."

Without Red Cloud's agreement, the treaty was worthless. That summer the War Department gave in to his demands and ordered the evacuation of Forts Reno, Phil Kearny, and C. F. Smith. As soon as the soldiers had packed their gear and marched out of the forts, Red Cloud's warriors rode in and triumphantly burned every building to the ground.

Red Cloud waited a while longer. Finally, on November 6, he showed up at Fort Laramie to sign the treaty himself. He had fought for several years to preserve his people's hunting grounds. Now the soldiers were gone. The forts were destroyed. The Bozeman Trail was closed. And the Powder River

22

Red Cloud (front row, second from left) with a delegation of tribal leaders in Washington, D.C., 1870. Altogether, Red Cloud journeyed to Washington eight times to negotiate for Sioux interests.

country would be Indian land forever.

Red Cloud had won his war. He was the first Indian leader in the West to win a war with the United States—and the last.

Red Cloud had promised never to make war again, and he kept that promise. He moved with his followers to the Great Sioux Reservation, where he would live for the rest of his eighty-seven years.

But there were other chiefs who refused to sign the treaty of 1868, among them influential leaders like Sitting Bull of the Hunkpapa Sioux and Two Moon of the Northern Cheyennes. They let it be known that they had not burned the white man's forts and closed his road to become reservation Indians, living on handouts from Washington. They had

fought to remain free. They stayed outside the boundaries of the new reservation, pitching their camps in the valleys of the Powder River country and living in the old way by hunting the buffalo. In their eyes, Red Cloud had surrendered to the whites by agreeing to a reservation. He had lost their respect. "The white people have put bad medicine over Red Cloud's eyes," said Sitting Bull, "to make him see everything and anything they please."

Red Cloud shrugged off the criticism. With a spacious reservation to live on, and with unrestricted hunting rights in the Powder River country, he believed that the Sioux could still control their own destiny. From then on, Red Cloud concentrated on protecting his people's interests. During the next few years, he made several trips to Washington to negotiate with government officials. He met twice with President Ulysses S. Grant, visited the Senate while it was in session, saw the sights and wonders of the great city, and witnessed at first hand the vast riches and power of the whites.

Once, he was taken on a guided tour of the U.S. Arsenal and shown more guns of different types than he had imagined the whole world contained. He was most impressed by a new cannon with a barrel almost wide enough for a man to crawl into. The gun was fired for him. Red Cloud watched as the great shell went screaming down the Potomac River. It could be seen skipping over the water four or five miles away. He said nothing, but the lesson was not lost on him.

Red Cloud's policy was to stay on good terms with the whites, yet hold fast to the old hunting and roving life, and never give it up. But he soon found that this was not possible. From the beginning, the Indians and the government argued bitterly about the treaty of 1868, which meant one thing to the chiefs who had signed it and another to the whites. The chiefs

Three generations. Red Cloud on the reservation
with his son and granddaughter.

insisted that they had not been told truthfully what the sixteen
articles of that treaty really said. They claimed they had been
lied to and deceived. "I signed a treaty of peace," Red Cloud
told the Secretary of the Interior, "but it was not this treaty.
This one is all lies!"

Lies or not, the treaty of 1868 didn't stay in effect for long.
Within a few years, warfare had broken out again. By 1876
the Sioux had been forced to give up the Powder River country
they had fought so hard to save, and to surrender the sacred
Black Hills region inside the boundaries of the Great Sioux

25

Red Cloud in old age

Reservation. After that, the reservation continued to shrink as much of the remaining land was sold off to white home-steaders.

Red Cloud had refused to take any part in the Sioux War of 1876, advising his followers to declare themselves peaceful and stay close to their reservation agency. His glimpses of the white man's world and strength had convinced him that armed resistance was futile. He realized now that his people were only a handful compared to the whites.

Even so, he continued his struggle to defend Sioux interests. In the years following the war, Red Cloud stubbornly opposed the sale of reservation lands. Meanwhile, he became an angry and persistent critic of the government agents sent from Washington to run the reservation, charging them with graft, corruption, and incompetence. In 1881 after a long feud with an agent named V. T. McGillycuddy, Red Cloud was ousted as the official chief of the Oglalas. McGillycuddy himself stripped the aging chief of his title at a public meeting. "Red Cloud, you have been mean and insolent," McGillycuddy told him. "Because you have defied your agent and insulted the Great Father, I now break you of your chieftainship. You are no longer chief of the Oglalas. Go to your tipi!"

Red Cloud's influence among his own people was also declining. As he grew more cautious and conservative in his later years, many of the younger Sioux rejected his leadership and judged him harshly. They felt he had sold out to the white man. "What can we do?" Red Cloud had asked. "The Great Father is all-powerful. His people fill the whole earth. We must do as he says."

By the time Red Cloud died in 1909, feeble and half blind, the Great Sioux Reservation had been split up into five smaller reservations and the roving life of the hunting bands was gone forever. Red Cloud had won his war, but he had lost the battle to preserve the Sioux's way of life.

"Our nation is melting away like the snow on the sides of the hills where the sun is warm," he once told the whites, "while your people are like blades of grass in the spring when summer is coming."

Satanta

SATANTA

I love to roam over the prairies. There I feel free and happy, but when we settle down, we grow pale and die.

In 1864 a government physician visited the southern plains to vaccinate the Indians against smallpox. "I have been two weeks among the Kiowas, about forty miles up the Arkansas River," he wrote. "I was four days in Satanta's, or White Bear's, village, who is, I believe, their principal chief. He is a fine-looking Indian, very energetic and sharp as a briar. He and all his people treated me with much friendship. I ate my meals three times a day with him in his lodge. He puts on a great deal of style, spreads a carpet for his guests to sit on. . . . He has a brass French horn which he blew vigorously when the meals were ready."

A few months later, Satanta used his French horn for a different purpose. In November 1864 the U.S. Army dispatched 350 volunteer troops commanded by Kit Carson to punish the Kiowas for their raids against white settlers in Texas. Carson and his men found themselves on the defensive when they were confronted by a thousand Kiowa and Comanche warriors. As the troopers retreated, there was much confusion. A bugler kept sounding the advance, and the soldiers milled about, unsure of their orders. The bugler was Satanta, blowing his dinner horn on the battlefield.

No one who met Satanta ever forgot him. A brawny, barrel-chested man with big shoulders and a bulldog chin, he stood well over six feet in his moccasins. Like his father, he lived in a flaming red tipi. On important occasions, and on the war-path, he wore brilliant red paint on his face and body, and he carried red streamers on his medicine lance.

His tribe was not a large one, numbering fewer than two thousand people, but the Kiowas were famous for their vast herds of horses and for the fighting spirit of their warriors. With their allies, the Comanches, the Kiowas ruled the southern plains. Their hunting grounds stretched from the Arkansas River in present-day Kansas south into the Texas Panhandle and sprawled across parts of those areas known today as Oklahoma, Colorado, and New Mexico. When Satanta was born in 1820, the only white settlements in this region were a few widely scattered army and fur-trading posts. The empty grasslands seemed to go on forever, and the world of the Kiowas was still wild and free.

Like all Kiowa youngsters, Satanta grew up on horseback. By the time he was five, he had his own pony. Before he was ten, he was galloping across the prairie, clinging to his pony with only his knees, leaving his hands free for his bow and arrow. With practice, he could fire twenty arrows as fast as a man armed with a musket could get off one shot and reload.

When he was fourteen or fifteen, he began to go along with Kiowa raiding parties that rode deep into Texas and Mexico. The raiders might be gone for months. They returned home with hundreds of stolen horses and mules, and often with

Indian Warfare. Frederic Remington's painting captures the superb horsemanship of the plains Indians. While cavalrymen fire from the distance, mounted warriors rescue a wounded comrade.
THE THOMAS GILCREASE INSTITUTE OF AMERICAN HISTORY AND ART, TULSA, OKLAHOMA

captive children who were adopted and raised as full members of the tribe.

Satanta showed such promise as a war leader that a famous old warrior named Black Horse gave him his shield. It was decorated with strips of red cloth on one side and yellow on the other, and it had the head of a whooping crane fastened to it. Painted on the center of the shield was a sun with two rings around it. Kiowa shields were made of several layers of tough buffalo hide, but a warrior relied more for protection on his shield's medicine—its magical powers. Black Horse had tested his shield's powers many times, and it had always kept him from harm. Soon after he gave the shield to Satanta, he was killed in a skirmish with some enemies.

31

From then on, Satanta carried that shield in every battle he ever fought. He had it with him in Mexico when a vaquero roped him and galloped off, dragging Satanta behind him. He would have been dragged to death if two other Kiowa warriors hadn't rescued him. He believed that the shield saved his life more than once, and that its powerful medicine helped him succeed as both a warrior and a chief.

As Satanta rose to leadership in his tribe, the Kiowas faced a growing threat to their control of the southern plains. For decades they had been fighting first the Spanish settlers on both sides of the Rio Grande, and later the Texans, who had taken some of their best hunting lands. By the 1840s thousands of emigrants bound for California were demanding the right to cross Kiowa territory as they traveled west along the Santa Fe Trail.

The invasion reached a peak in 1859, when more than ninety thousand emigrants passed over the great trail with their creaking wagons and their herds of bawling cattle. At one time, the Kiowas and Comanches had been willing to let the whites pass through their country unmolested. Now some emigrants were staking out farms and ranches on Indian land. Endless trains of covered wagons were scaring off the buffalo, and the emigrants' cattle were stripping the grasslands bare. Kiowa and Comanche warriors began to strike at travelers and settlers alike, ambushing wagon trains and raiding isolated ranches and stage stations. By the 1860s a state of war existed throughout the Kiowa-Comanche domain, from the Arkansas River south to the Rio Grande.

The Kiowas had a number of strong and willful leaders, and they could not agree on how to deal with the whites. As the chiefs met around the council fire, the tribe became divided into two opposing factions. Chiefs Kicking Bird and

Stumbling Bear feared the power of the U.S. Army. They argued that the Kiowas must remain at peace with the whites if they were to survive as a tribe. Other chiefs, including Satanta, Lone Wolf, and Satank, wanted to fight for every inch of land. Satanta was willing to take part in peace meetings, but he did not trust the whites. "The good Indian, he that listens to the white man, gets nothing," he said. "The independent Indian is the only one rewarded."

In April 1867 Army General Winfield Scott Hancock invited the Kiowa chiefs to a council at Fort Dodge, Kansas. Kicking Bird and Stumbling Bear spoke for the peaceful faction of the tribe. Satanta spoke for the others, and at the time, he seemed willing enough to compromise. He called on the sun to bear witness that he would "talk straight." Looking out over the prairie, he remarked that it was large and good. He did not wish to see it stained with blood. General Hancock was so pleased with the speech, he presented Satanta with the uniform coat, sash, and hat of a U.S. Army major-general.

But as the whites discovered, Satanta was always full of surprises. A few weeks later, he paid another visit to General Hancock. Decked out in his new uniform, he led a raid against Fort Dodge, stealing the horses belonging to Company B, Seventh Cavalry, and doffing his plumed hat in a parting salute to the soldiers who pursued him.

In October 1867 Congress sent a peace commission west to settle the Indian problem once and for all. The commissioners wanted to negotiate new treaties with the southern plains tribes. They planned to assign each tribe to a permanent reservation, away from white settlements and travel routes. The Indians would be provided with tools and cattle so they could become farmers and ranchers.

The talks were held in a beautiful grove of cottonwood trees

Lone Wolf, a leader of the Kiowa's militant war faction. He refused to sign the Treaty of Medicine Lodge Creek, and he joined the insurgents during the warfare of 1874–75. Shipped off to Florida as a prisoner of war, he died in 1879, a year after he returned home. He was photographed on a visit to Washington, D.C., in 1872.

Kicking Bird sided with the Kiowa's peace faction. He refused to take part in hostilities, urging his followers to stay on the reservation and declare themselves peaceful. He died in 1875—apparently poisoned by a resentful tribesman. He was photographed at Fort Dodge, Kansas, in 1868.

on Medicine Lodge Creek in southern Kansas. It was one of the biggest peace councils ever, with some five thousand Kiowas, Comanches, Southern Cheyennes, and Southern Arapahos camped along the wooded banks of the creek. The leading chiefs in all their finery sat on rows of logs, facing the commissioners in their black suits and army officers in their dress uniforms. Interpreters, soldiers, and warriors watched from the background. A brass peace pipe was passed in unbroken silence. After each participant had taken a puff, the council began.

When it was Satanta's turn to speak, he stood up and shook

INDIAN LODGE AT MEDICINE CREEK, KANSAS—SCENE OF THE LATE INDIAN PEACE COUNCIL.—Sketched by J. Howland.—[See Page 725.]

COUNCIL AT MEDICINE CREEK LODGE WITH THE KIOWA AND COMANCHE INDIANS.—Sketched by J. Howland.—[See Page 725.]

The great peace council on Medicine Lodge Creek, Kansas, attracted newspaper and magazine reporters and artists from all over the country. These sketches appeared in *Harper's Weekly* on November 16, 1867. (Note that the editors of the magazine mixed up the name of Medicine Lodge Creek.)

hands with each commissioner. Hanging from his neck was a silver medal bearing a profile of President James Buchanan (1857–1861). He described himself as the white man's friend, but he did not mince words:

"All the land south of the Arkansas River belongs to the Kiowas and the Comanches, and I don't want to give any of it away. I love the land and the buffalo and will not part with it. I don't want any of the medicine lodges [churches and schools] within the country. I want the children raised as I was.

"I have heard that you intend to settle us on a reservation near the mountains. I don't want to settle. I love to roam over the prairies. There I feel free and happy, but when we settle down, we grow pale and die.

"A long time ago this land belonged to our fathers, but when I go up the river I see camps of soldiers on its banks. These soldiers cut down my timber. They kill my buffalo. And when I see that, I feel as though my heart will burst with sorrow."

Satanta had rehearsed his speech with care, and he spoke for a long time. When he finished, the Kiowas shouted their approval. The commissioners were silent. The newspaper reporters, who had come from all over the country to cover the peace talks, were impressed. They began to call Satanta "the Orator of the Plains."

As the talks continued, the commissioners reminded the chiefs of the vast power of the Great Father in Washington. If the chiefs failed to cooperate, there was the threat of renewed war that could destroy their tribes. Army General William Tecumseh Sherman told the chiefs that no matter what they wanted, they had to give up the old ways and follow the ways of the white man. They could not stop the roads and rails from coming into their territory. They would have to learn to live like white settlers, from farming and ranching. "You can no more stop this," said Sherman, "than you can stop the sun or moon. You must submit and do the best you can."

After several days, the Medicine Lodge Treaty was ready for signing. Under its terms, the Kiowas and Comanches would give up much of their territory and settle on a reservation in Indian Territory (now Oklahoma). However, they would be allowed to hunt on their former lands in southern Kansas and the Texas Panhandle. In return, they would receive yearly payments of food, clothing, and other supplies.

Several chiefs refused to make their marks on the treaty. But most of them did sign—including Satanta. Perhaps they felt they had little to lose. Although they were expected to live on a reservation, they could leave it whenever they wished to follow the buffalo. They certainly didn't intend to become farmers. Some chiefs believed that since they had objected strongly to certain provisions of the treaty, those sections did not apply to them.

After the signing, gifts were handed out, as was customary at peace councils. Among the gifts were some shiny new pistols, and the young warriors were eager to test them. As it turned out, the pistols were faulty. Every one of them blew up the first time it was fired.

That winter, the treaty-signing Kiowas and Comanches settled on their shared reservation in Indian Territory. Kiowa hunters continued to ride west into the Texas Panhandle, seeking buffalo to feed their families. Often they returned empty-handed. Buffalo were getting scarce. White hunters armed with long-range rifles had been slaughtering entire herds for meat, for hides, and often just for the sport of it.

The supplies promised by the government were disappointing. The Kiowas were accustomed to plenty of fresh meat, and they resented the meager government handouts of salt pork and cornmeal. They fed the cornmeal to their horses.

A mood of anger and frustration began to spread through the reservation. Many of the tribespeople felt swindled by the Medicine Lodge Treaty. Hundreds of young men slipped away to join the nontreaty bands still living freely out on the plains, and before long, the frontier was in turmoil again. Kiowa and Comanche war parties rode south into Texas to raid settlements for food, horses, and guns. To the north, Cheyenne and Arapaho warriors left their reservation to strike at settlers in Kansas and Colorado.

General Sherman, military commander of the region, retaliated by suspending part of the treaty. Indians would no longer be allowed to hunt outside the boundaries of their reservations. They could not follow the migrating buffalo herds, even if they were desperate for meat. "We have selected and provided reservations for all, off the great road [the Santa Fe Trail]," said Sherman. "All who cling to their old hunting grounds are hostile and will remain so till killed off."

The Kiowas were warned to give up the warpath. They were urged to follow the example of the Caddos and Wichitas, who had long since settled down as farmers. Satanta wanted to laugh. The Wichitas grew corn, he said, because they were too fat and lazy to hunt buffalo. They scratched in the dirt like women. The Kiowas regarded farming as women's work, not a job for hunters and warriors. Besides, much of the land they had been given was unfit for farming.

Around the Kiowa campfires, the young men talked constantly of the whites who seemed to be pressing in on them from all directions. Each time they went out on the plains,

The Attack. In this Frederic Remington painting,
warriors attack a frontier settlement.

they found more ranches, more fences, and more white buffalo hunters. They had heard that the steel tracks for a new
Iron Horse would be coming directly into their country. Once
the railroad arrived, the buffalo were bound to disappear
completely.

The Kiowa chiefs were still debating, still arguing for or
against peace. Kicking Bird again called for patience and co-
operation. Satanta was defiant. With other rebellious chiefs,
he continued to lead raids into Texas.

In May 1871 a band of Kiowa and Comanche warriors attacked a wagon train carrying supplies to Fort Richardson,
Texas. The Indians surrounded the freight train, killed seven
teamsters, looted the wagons, then rode off. A few days later,
several Kiowa chiefs showed up at Fort Sill, their reservation
agency, to draw their weekly food rations. Lawrie Tatum, the

agent in charge of the reservation, called the chiefs into his office. He asked if they knew anything about the attack near Fort Richardson. Satanta immediately spoke up:

"Yes, I led that raid....I have repeatedly asked for arms and ammunition [for hunting], which you have not furnished. I have made many other requests which have not been granted. You do not listen to me talk. The white people are preparing to build a railroad through our country, which will not be permitted. Some years ago they took us by the hair and pulled us here close to Texas, where we have to fight them."

Angrily, Satanta listed his many complaints. "On account of these grievances," he continued, "a short time ago I took about one hundred of my warriors to Texas, with the chiefs Satank, Eagle Heart, Big Bow, Big Tree, and Fast Bear..."

Satank broke in, interrupting Satanta and warning him not to go on. But Satanta persisted. "We found a mule train, which we captured, and killed seven of the men. Three of our men got killed, but we are willing to call it even. It is all over now, and it is not necessary to say much more about it....If any other Indian claims the honor of leading that party, he will be lying to you. I led it myself."

After the chiefs left his office, Tatum reported the confession to the commanding officer of Fort Sill, who in turn notified General Sherman. Satanta, Satank, and Big Tree were arrested and hustled off to the guardhouse. Sherman ordered that they be sent back to Texas to stand trial for murder. Handcuffed and hobbled with chains, Satanta and Big Tree were put in one wagon, Satank in another.

As the wagons left the gates of Fort Sill, Satank called out to his fellow prisoners: "I am a chief and a warrior, and too old to be treated as a child." He pointed down the road and shouted, "I shall never go beyond that tree!" The soldiers who

41

Satank, or Sitting Bear, chief of the Society of the Ten Bravest.
At the age of sixty-nine, Satank was still leading raids into Texas.
Arrested with Satanta and Big Tree, and charged with murder, he
deliberately provoked his guards and was shot down.

Big Tree was imprisoned with Satanta in Texas. Paroled in 1873, he was arrested again a year later. After his release in 1875, he settled down with his followers on Rainy Mountain Creek, where he became a deacon and Sunday school teacher at the local Baptist church.

were guarding the prisoners ignored him, since none of them spoke Kiowa.

Satank was chief of the Kaitsenko—the Society of the Ten Bravest—an ancient Kiowa military order. Crouching in his wagon, he began to chant the death song of the Kaitsenko. When his song ended, he pulled his blanket over his head, as though he were grieving. Unseen by the guards, he gnawed the flesh from his hands until he could wring off his handcuffs. Then he pulled out a hidden knife, leaped up, and attacked the two soldiers riding with him, stabbing one and grabbing his rifle. Before he could fire, he was shot down by the other guards. His body was left by the roadside as the wagons continued.

Satanta and Big Tree were taken to the frontier town of Jacksboro, Texas, where they were tried for first-degree murder. Speaking to the jury of local ranchers and cowboys, the prosecuter called Satanta "the arch fiend of treachery and blood . . . the promoter of strife, the breaker of treaties signed by his own hand." The chiefs were found guilty and sentenced to death by hanging.

The trial caused a great outcry. Humanitarian groups in the East protested that the sentences were too harsh and would only incite Kiowa reprisals. Reservation agent Lawrie Tatum suggested that the chiefs be imprisoned rather than executed, and the governor of Texas agreed. Satanta and Big Tree were sent to the Texas State Prison at Huntsville to serve life terms at hard labor.

When General Sherman heard the news, he was furious. "Satanta ought to have been hung, and that would have ended the trouble," he said. "I know these Kiowas well enough to see that they will be everlastingly pleading for his release. He should never be released. I hope the War Department will

General William Tecumseh Sherman, of Civil War fame, commanded the U.S. Army during its final years of warfare with the western tribes. Sherman advocated a hardline approach to Indian affairs, calling the tribes "the enemies of our race and of our civilization."

never consent to his return to his tribe."

Sherman's worst fears were to be realized. Back east, pro-Indian groups called for the release of Satanta and Big Tree, arguing that their imprisonment could only make matters worse with the plains tribes. In Washington, the Indian Bureau urged clemency on grounds that the chiefs had committed an act of war, not murder.

Meanwhile, the Kiowas themselves were working behind the scenes. In 1873 a delegation of Kiowa chiefs traveled to Washington to meet with the Commissioner of Indian Affairs. They reminded him that Satanta and Big Tree were the war chiefs of the tribe. As long as they remained in prison, many of the young warriors would continue to fight the Texans.

Another plea came from Satanta's elderly father, Red Tipi. "I am a poor old man," he told white officials. "I want you to pity me and give up my son. The Indians love their children as much as the white people do theirs. Take pity on me and gladden my heart by the immediate release of my son. Never again will we raid upon Texas."

Governor Edmund Davis of Texas finally agreed to release the two chiefs in October 1873, after they had served two years. But he warned them that they were being freed on parole. If they set foot off the reservation, they would be sent back to prison.

Satanta had promised to abandon the warpath. He moved back into his red-painted tipi, with its red streamers flying from the smoke holes at the top. He gave his red medicine lance to his friend White Cowbird and his famous buffalo-hide shield to his son. Without his shield and lance, he could never again lead warriors into battle, for they were the medicine that had always protected him. He claimed he had no wish to be a warrior or a chief any longer. The famous Orator of the Plains seemed a changed man. "Whatever the white man thinks best," he said, "I want my people to do."

But it was too late for that. Indians and whites alike were being swept along by events that would allow no peace. The Plains Indians had always depended on the buffalo for their livelihood and their self-respect. Now buffalo were being slaughtered by the millions. A new breed of white hunter had appeared on the plains. These men stripped the animal of its valuable hide and left the rest of the carcass to rot under the sun. Because of a new tanning process that turned the hides into expensive leather, a single hide was now worth about three dollars—more than a factory worker earned in a week. Armed with high-powered rifles, the hide hunters did nothing but kill and skin buffalo from morning to night. By the time Satanta and Big Tree were paroled in 1873, so many buffalo had been wiped out that Kiowa and Comanche hunters could

46

Buffalo hides purchased by the firm of Rath & Wright in Dodge City, Kansas, 1874. There were said to be forty thousand hides in the pile.

no longer feed their families. That winter, many of the Indians were forced to eat their ponies.

As the hide hunters worked their way across the plains, the Indians came to hate them with a bitter hate. In 1874 war parties of Kiowas, Comanches, Cheyennes, and Arapahos began to attack the hunters' camps in the Texas Panhandle. Soon their fury spread to include other whites, wherever they found them. Warriors struck at ranches, trading posts, and wagon trains in Kansas, Colorado, New Mexico, and Texas. Texas newspapers charged that Satanta and Big Tree, just released from prison, were leading some of the raids.

General Sherman ordered all Indians to report to their reservations at once and register by name. Army officers would hold weekly roll calls. Those who did not answer to their names would be declared hostile and hunted down. Some three thousand cavalrymen fanned out across the plains to find the hostile bands.

Many Kiowas, led by Kicking Bird, the patient advocate of peace, refused to have anything to do with this latest conflict. They declared themselves peaceful by reporting to their agency at Fort Sill and answering the roll calls. Other Kiowa bands, rallied by militant chiefs like Lone Wolf, scattered across the plains and ran from the army troops. They were pursued by soldiers armed with repeating rifles, Gatling guns, and howitzers. The army kept up the pressure, never giving the Indians a chance to hunt for food or to rest. As the summer of 1874 ended, the hostile bands began to come out of hiding and gave themselves up at Fort Sill.

Satanta always claimed that he was not involved in the hostilities that summer. He admitted that he and Big Tree had left the Kiowa reservation, but only to hunt for buffalo. When fighting broke out, the two chiefs—who were still on parole— were afraid to return to their reservation agency at Fort Sill. They decided to hide out in the Red Hills until the conflict had ended.

In October, Satanta and Big Tree turned themselves in to military authorities. They insisted that they had not taken part in any fighting. Even so, by leaving their reservation without permission, they had broken the terms of their parole. They were arrested, shackled in irons, and sent as prisoners to Fort Sill.

Several officials came to their defense. The Commissioner of Indian Affairs, Edward Smith, argued that Satanta and Big Tree were guilty of nothing more than temporary panic. The

Holding a bow and arrow, and wearing his
prized medal of President James Buchanan,
Satanta poses for a frontier photographer.

superintendent of the Plains tribes, Enoch Hoag, reported that both chiefs had remained peaceful. "No evidence has reached this office of any hostility on their part," said Hoag. "They have recently, without compulsion, voluntarily surrendered to the military, and are confined at Fort Sill. I recommend official clemency in their case."

General Sherman did not favor clemency. He had always regarded Satanta as a menace, and he demanded that the chief be returned to prison. His recommendation was approved by President Grant.

Satanta was sent back to the Texas State Prison to serve a life sentence. Big Tree was treated more leniently. He was held for a few months at Fort Sill and then released. Meanwhile, twenty-five Kiowa and Comanche warriors had been singled out as leaders of the hostile bands. They were shipped off to a military prison in Florida.

Seven years had passed since the Kiowas had signed the Medicine Lodge Treaty. Since then, they had lost most of their hunting grounds. Nearly all of their great leaders were imprisoned. And the buffalo they had fought to save had vanished from the plains.

Satanta languished in prison for four more years, bitterly protesting his innocence. In August 1878 the prison superintendent reported: "Satanta is here in declining health and very feeble. If he remains here he cannot live long. Will heartily second any effort for his release."

A month later, Satanta asked a deputy marshal if he would ever be released. The answer was no. The next day, Satanta was admitted to the prison hospital. On September 11, 1878 he threw himself headfirst from a second-story hospital balcony and died a few hours later. He was fifty-eight.

SATANTA

In 1963 Satanta's grandson, James Auchiah, received permission to move the chief's remains from Texas to Fort Sill, Oklahoma, in the heart of the old Kiowa hunting grounds. Satanta was buried again in the post cemetery, this time with full military honors.

Quanah Parker

QUANAH PARKER

This was a pretty country you took away from us.

They rode out of nowhere in quick attacks, stampeding horses and killing sentries with silent arrows. Then they vanished into the tall grass as swiftly as they had come.

Time and again during the early 1870s, Comanche warriors struck at the army's blue-coated cavalry troops, then lost themselves in the Texas Panhandle. The raiders were led by a young man riding a coal-black racing pony. His face was smeared with black war paint. His black hair hung in two braids like ropes over his shoulders. And his eyes were grayish-blue. The Comanches called him Quanah. The Texans knew him as the notorious half-breed war chief, Quanah Parker.

His mother, Cynthia Ann Parker, had been born on the Texas frontier. At the age of nine, she was abducted by a Comanche war party that raided her parents' homestead, killing most of the adults. Like other captive white children, Cynthia was adopted into the tribe. Soon she was speaking the Comanche language and enjoying tough buffalo meat.

In her teens she became the wife of Peta Nacona, a young

warrior who would eventually lead his own band. Her first child was born around 1847, probably in the springtime, when prairie flowers were blooming everywhere. She named the baby boy Quanah, the Comanche word for "fragrant" or "sweet-smelling." Later she had another son, Pecos, or Peanut, and a daughter, Topsannah, or Prairie Flower.

By all accounts, Cynthia Ann was happy in her new life. Years later, some American army officers traveling through Comanche country met the yellow-haired, blue-eyed young woman and offered to pay a ransom for her freedom. She refused. She now had a family to care for, and no wish to return to the old life she barely remembered.

At one time, the Comanches were the largest and most powerful tribe in the West, some twenty thousand strong. With their Kiowa allies, they controlled a vast territory centered in Texas. Feared as warriors and famous as horsemen, they were said to own more horses than any other tribe. An ordinary warrior owned perhaps 250 horses, a war chief as many as 1,500.

For more than a century, Comanche war parties had been riding south along a trail marked by horses' bones to raid Spanish settlements hundreds of miles inside Mexico. As American settlers began to filter into Texas, they too became the target of Comanche raids. By the time Texas won independence from Mexico in 1836, the Texans and the Comanches were sworn enemies.

The Texas Rangers had been organized to fight the Comanches on their own terms. They answered Indian raids with lightning attacks of their own, burning encampments and running off horses deep inside Comanche territory. The Comanches replied by sending out war parties to kill and scalp

A Comanche encampment. The wooden poles that formed the skeleton of a tipi left a hole at the top for ventilation, allowing smoke to escape when a fire was lighted.

white settlers in revenge. Raids and counterraids became a way of life on the Texas frontier. Long after Texas joined the United States in 1845, the Comanches still made a distinction between Texans and other Americans. Even when they signed treaties with the United States, most Comanches refused to make peace with Texas.

Quanah was still a boy when a surprise raid by Texas Rangers brought disaster to his family. In December 1860 a force of forty Rangers and twenty-one cavalrymen attacked an encampment of the Nacona band, led by Quanah's father. Quanah was out on the plains that day, hunting buffalo with his father and the other men. When they returned to their burned and smoldering camp with its scattered, tumbled corpses, they found the survivors wailing and moaning in grief. Quanah's mother was gone, along with his little sister, Prairie Flower.

The Rangers had recognized Cynthia Ann as the girl carried

off by the Indians so many years before. With her baby, she was returned to the Parker family she had not seen for twenty-five years. The Parkers welcomed her back joyfully and did everything they could to help ease her return to civilization. But she no longer thought of herself as a Parker or even a Texan. She was a Naduah, a Comanche woman, separated from her husband, her two sons, and her people, who were still out on the prairie. When she tried to escape, her bewildered relatives put her under guard. Then her little girl died of a disease, and the grieving Cynthia Ann felt she had nothing else to live for. Years later, Quanah found out that his mother had starved herself to death.

Cynthia Ann Parker, Quanah's mother. After living with the Comanches for twenty-five years, she was recaptured by Texas Rangers and returned to the Parker family in Texas. Four years later, she starved herself to death.

His father died of an infected wound soon after the Rangers' raid. Then his brother, Pecos, fell prey to some disease. In quick succession, the boy had lost his entire family and had to depend on the charity of other band members.

Quanah was still a teenager when he left the Nacona band to join the proud and independent Kwahadis, the most remote and warlike of all the Comanche bands. They lived far to the west of the other bands, on the barren, windswept ranges of the Staked Plains on the Texas Panhandle. They were called Kwahadis—"Sun Shades on Their Backs"—because they rode about holding buffalo-hide parasols. The Kwahadis kept their distance when the U.S. government sent a peace commission west to sign new treaties with the plains tribes in October 1867. At Medicine Lodge Creek in Kansas, most of the leading Comanche and Kiowa chiefs agreed to settle on a reservation in Indian Territory. The Kwahadis refused to take part in the peace talks. Quanah was about twenty years old at the time, and fiercely loyal to his adopted band. "My people are not going to live on a reservation," he told a friend. "Let the white chiefs know that the Kwahadis are warriors. We'll surrender when the blue-coats come and whip us on the Staked Plains."

Several thousand Comanches and Kiowas did settle on the new reservation, but they soon regretted it. To a people who were accustomed to roaming freely, reservation life seemed stagnant and confining. There was never enough to eat. The men resented the government's efforts to make obedient farmers out of them. Within months, dissatisfied tribespeople began to drift away. They were willing to accept government rations during the hard winter months, but with the promise of summer, they rode back to the plains to follow the buffalo.

Some bands never visited the reservation agency at Fort Sill. They wandered as they pleased, ignoring reservation boundaries, hunting and raiding as usual. The government soon realized that the Indians could be kept on the reservation only by force. "The settlers and emigrants must be protected," said General of the Army Ulysses S. Grant, "even if the extermination of every Indian tribe is necessary to secure such a result." Grant ordered the army to round up every hostile band and put an end to the raiding once and for all.

The Kwahadis were the largest of the hostile bands, and they welcomed into their ranks the growing numbers of restless young warriors who came to join them. They boasted that they had never signed a treaty with anyone. They had never once set foot on the reservation. They were the band that the whites blamed most for the continuing raids against frontier settlements.

By the early 1870s the Kwahadis were fighting a guerrilla war against cavalry troops led by Ranald Mackenzie, a tough young colonel who had lost a finger in the Civil War. The Indians called him Three Fingers. Quanah was beginning to earn a great reputation as a warrior. He fought alongside Bull Bear, the leading Kwahadi chief, and as he displayed judgment and daring, he organized war parties of his own. Mackenzie soon learned to recognize the tall, powerfully built young warrior who led so many surprise raids against his troops.

As Mackenzie's cavalrymen probed the Staked Plains, they became as much the hunted as the hunters. They found themselves in unknown, untracked country, chasing an enemy that appeared and vanished like the prairie winds. Quanah and his warriors never stayed in one place long enough to fight a pitched battle. They would shadow the cavalry columns and attack suddenly—sweeping over the top of a ridge, swirling around the surprised troopers, then dissolving into the grass-

Ranald Mackenzie wearing the star of a brigadier general. Called "Three Fingers" by the Comanches, Mackenzie pursued Quanah and his warriors across the Staked Plains of the Texas Panhandle.

lands. Sometimes the Kwahadis raided by moonlight, ringing cowbells and flapping buffalo robes as they charged through the army camp and stampeded the horses. Once they even put an arrow into Mackenzie. The cavalrymen patrolled constantly, scouring the plains and keeping Quanah on the run, but they were never able to defeat him.

The army was having better luck with its campaign against the other hostile bands. By the beginning of 1874 most of the rebel Comanches had drifted back to the reservation, and for a while there was a lull in the fighting. The Kwahadis remained free and untamed on the Staked Plains. They might have held out for years, but the army had now gained a useful ally. The fate of the southern Plains tribes would be settled not in battle with the U.S. Cavalry, but by white buffalo-hide hunters who were shooting their way south.

Up north in Kansas, most of the buffalo had already been killed off. Long stretches of Kansas prairie were littered with

Hunting the Buffalo. This 1873 engraving by W. W. Rice depicts a traditional Indian buffalo hunt. The buffalo was more than just meat. It supplied nearly everything the plains Indians needed—from leather for their tipis to bones for their cups and spoons.

rotting carcasses and half-bared bones left behind by the hide men. Now the hunters were moving south toward the Texas Panhandle. The Medicine Lodge Treaty had forbidden white hunters to enter the Panhandle, but the army made no effort to stop them. Many army officers believed that the best way to keep the Indians on their reservations was to destroy their basic food supply. "Let them kill, skin, and sell until the buffalo is exterminated," said General Philip Sheridan, "as it is the

Trail of the hide hunters. Between 1872 and 1874, nearly four million buffalo were killed by white hide hunters armed with powerful long-range rifles. The extermination of the buffalo doomed the plains Indians' way of life and forced them to stay on the reservation.

only way to bring lasting peace and allow civilization to advance."

On the reservations and off, the tribes were enraged by the slaughter of the buffalo herds. They knew that when the buffalo were gone, their way of life would be doomed. From all over the southern plains, angry warriors rallied to declare an all-out war against the hide hunters. Comanches from several bands were joined at a war council by Kiowas, Cheyennes, and

Arapahos. They agreed to strike first at the big hide hunters' base at Adobe Walls, an old trading post in the Texas Panhandle. Bull Bear, the leading Kwahadi chief, lay dying of pneumonia, and Quanah had taken his place. The warriors picked him to lead their massive assault on Adobe Walls.

Just before dawn on June 27, 1874 the Indians launched their attack. About seven hundred warriors came thundering out of the darkness. They swept toward the trading post and circled around it, hurling lances, pounding on doors, firing through windows. "We charged pretty fast on our horses, throwing up dust high," Quanah recalled. "There were many prairie dog holes, and I saw men and horses roll over and over. Some warriors who were up ahead drove off the white man's horses. I got up onto an adobe house with another Comanche. We poked holes through the roof to shoot."

Quanah led several charges that day as the Indians tried to break into the post, but each time they were driven back by volleys of rifle fire. During one charge, Quanah's horse was shot out from under him. As he dove for cover, a bullet creased his shoulder. He saved himself by crawling behind a dead buffalo and crouching there until a fellow warrior rescued him.

There were only twenty-eight hunters barricaded inside the post, but they had a big advantage. They were armed with powerful long-range buffalo rifles, equipped with telescopic sights. They could knock a warrior off his horse from half a mile away. As the Indians' casualties mounted, Quanah decided to call off his warriors and end the battle.

The Indians withdrew, taking with them the bodies of fifteen fallen comrades. Left behind were twelve more Indian dead whose bodies could not be recovered. The hunters had lost three men, and when the last Indian was out of sight, they had their revenge. They chopped off the heads of the dead warriors and stuck them on the pickets of the post corral.

After the defeat at Adobe Walls, the Indians gave vent to their fury. Small bands of warriors scattered across the plains, ambushing stage coaches, burning ranch houses, killing buffalo hunters, and causing bloody havoc from Texas to Colorado. Alarmed by the violent uprising, the government issued an ultimatum: all Indians must enroll at their reservation agencies or be attacked as hostile.

The army had been rushing reinforcements to Texas. Five cavalry columns, some three thousand well-armed troops, were sent out to hunt for the hostile bands and drive them back to Fort Sill. The Indians were in a state of panic and confusion. Many tribespeople submitted at once, registering at their reservations and declaring themselves peaceful. Others fled during the turmoil and went into hiding out on the plains. By mid-July, half the Comanches and Kiowas had abandoned the reservation to join the runaways. Quanah's defiant Kwahadis were still camped on the Staked Plains, where they had managed to preserve their freedom all along. They became the hard core of Indian resistance.

The army had learned that the best way to fight the Indians was to press after them, chasing them without letup, attacking at every opportunity and destroying everything they possessed. The runaways were not just warriors. There were entire families and bands out on the plains, and they were forced to keep moving with their children and infants, their old men and women, and their wounded. They had no chance to hunt for food, to repair their tattered clothing or ripped tipis, to rest themselves or their scrawny ponies. When the soldiers found an encampment and drove the Indians out, they burned their tipis, buffalo robes, arrows, and food stocks. Holes were

Indians on the Move. Engraving by John C. MacRae.

smashed in the bottoms of cooking kettles. Horses and mules were rounded up and shot.

As the summer ended, some of the rebel bands began to straggle into Fort Sill and give themselves up. Others held out through the bitter winter months of 1874 before they finally surrendered. They showed up at Fort Sill in ragged groups, shivering and demoralized, begging to be fed.

Quanah and his Kwahadis continued to resist. Trailed by Three Fingers Mackenzie, they fled deeper into the Staked Plains. By now, Mackenzie's soldiers knew the country well. They had discovered every secret camping site, every hiding place, of the Kwahadis. That winter Quanah and his warriors fought two dozen skirmishes with the cavalrymen. They wore out most of their equipment. They moved camp every day. And they lived through the winter on nuts, grubs, and field mice.

In April government messengers flying truce flags sought out Quanah and delivered an ultimatum: if the Kwahadis gave themselves up, they would not be punished. Otherwise, none of them would live through the summer. Quanah realized that continuing warfare would mean suicide for all his people. He gathered the Kwahadis together, and on June 2, 1875, he led them into Fort Sill. They were the last band to surrender and the last Indians to live freely on the southern plains.

General Philip Sheridan, who had encouraged the slaughter of the buffalo, understood clearly why the Indians had fought so hard. "We took away their country and means of support," Sheridan said, "broke up their mode of living, their habits of life, introduced disease and decay among them. And it was for this and against this that they made war. Could anyone expect less?"

In 1875, Quanah spoke only a few words of English. He had never lived in a house, eaten at a table, or slept in a bed. During the next twenty years, he would become a wealthy rancher, the major stockholder in a railroad, and the friend of presidents and congressmen.

When he surrendered at Fort Sill, he knew he would have to leave the past behind him. The Comanches were a defeated people. Decades of warfare and disease had reduced their numbers until there were fewer than two thousand Comanches left to settle on the reservation. Their only hope now was to cooperate with the whites. Quanah had been a great Comanche war chief, but for the rest of his life, he would be a man of peace.

Any doubts about the Comanches' future were laid to rest in 1878. That fall they were given permission to leave the reservation for a buffalo hunt. Under the watchful eyes of a military escort, the entire tribe set out eagerly for the plains to the west. Scouts rode miles ahead of the main group, searching every stream bed and creek, probing every stand of trees. But there were no buffalo to be seen. The scouts found nothing but buffalo bones and skulls bleached white by the sun.

The people refused to turn back. They still believed that when the leaves fell, the buffalo would come pouring onto their southern ranges, as they always had come when winter winds blew down from the north. But the buffalo did not come. The Comanches pitched their tipis out on the plains and waited, still hoping. They waited until the snows fell and their food ran out. Only then would they agree to go back to the reservation. It had taken about six years for the hide hunters to wipe out the millions of buffalo that had ranged from Kansas southward into Texas.

Before long, great herds of longhorn cattle were grazing where the buffalo had roamed. Texas ranchers had started to

drive their herds through reservation lands on the way to markets in Kansas. Quanah and the other Comanche leaders insisted that the cattlemen pay for this privilege. They charged the ranchers a dollar a head for grazing rights, and with this income, the tribe began to build up its own herds of beef cattle.

Now that the Comanches had made their peace with the whites, Quanah set out on a personal mission. He had always wanted to meet his mother's family in Texas. He was given a pass that allowed him to leave the reservation, a hand-drawn map, and a letter from the reservation agent: "This young man is the son of Cynthia Ann Parker, and he is going to visit his mother's people. Please show him the road and help him as you can."

He rode off alone into the world of the whites and found his mother's uncle, Silas Parker, in eastern Texas. The Parker family welcomed him and made him feel at home. He stayed with them for several weeks, practicing his English, studying farming methods, and sleeping in his mother's bed.

When he returned to the reservation, Quanah threw himself into the affairs of his tribe. An able and energetic leader, he was soon recognized as the principal chief of the Comanches and their leading spokesman. He traveled frequently to Washington, where he shook hands with the President, met with members of Congress, and discussed Comanche concerns with the Commissioner of Indian Affairs. Back home, the once-defiant war chief was appointed chief judge of a three-man Court of Indian Offenses. He also served as deputy sheriff of Lawton, Oklahoma, a town near Fort Sill, and as president of his local school district.

A success as a politician, Quanah proved to be a shrewd businessman as well. He negotiated profitable leases with Texas

Buffalo bones. By the late 1870s, sun-bleached buffalo bones lay scattered all over the western plains.

cattlemen, allowing them to graze their herds on Comanche land, and they in turn advised him on his personal investments. He prospered as a rancher in his own right. His comfortable twelve-room ranch house, built for him by Texas cattle baron Burk Burnett, became known as the Comanche White House. People said that Quanah was the richest Indian in America.

He was certainly one of the best known. In 1901 he traveled to Washington to ride in President Theodore Roosevelt's inaugural procession. When Roosevelt visited Oklahoma five years later, he made a point of calling on his old friend, Quanah Parker, and the two men went hunting together.

Some Comanches charged that Quanah had sold out to the cattlemen and that he had allowed himself to become a willing mouthpiece of the white officials who actually ran the reservation. Despite the criticism, Quanah's popularity remained

high among his tribespeople. Most Comanches respected him for trying to protect their interests at a time when the tribe was powerless.

Although Quanah had an official title as principal chief of the Comanches, he had little authority. The tribe's affairs were controlled by Indian agents sent out from Washington. They held the real power. As chief, Quanah had to get along with every one of the fourteen white men who served as agents on the Comanche reservation between 1878 and his death in 1911.

Often he had to compromise, but when he felt strongly about an issue, he could be blunt and outspoken. He opposed all efforts to recruit Comanche men as members of U.S. Army cavalry battalions. "My people quit fighting long ago," he said, "and we have no desire to join anyone in war again."

He criticized the whites for their wasteful farming and ranching practices, which had turned vast stretches of grassland into arid mesquite-scrub prairie. Speaking at a Fourth of July picnic in Hobart, Oklahoma, in 1890, Quanah said: "We love the white man, but we fear your success. This was a pretty country you took away from us, but you see how dry it is now. It is only good for red ants, coyotes, and cattlemen."

He could also be gracious. In his dedication speech at Quanah, Texas, a town named after him in the heart of Comanche country, he said: "May the Great Spirit always smile on your new town. May the rain always fall in due season. In the warmth of the sunshine after the rain, may the earth yield bountifully for you. May peace and contentment dwell with you and your children forever. I am Quanah, and I say, thank you."

The last battle of Quanah's life took place in the halls of Congress during the 1890s, when he fought to save the res-

Quanah's twelve-room ranch house near Cache, Oklahoma. Known as the Comanche White House, it had twenty-two stars painted on the roof.
THE THOMAS GILCREASE INSTITUTE OF AMERICAN HISTORY AND ART, TULSA, OKLAHOMA

ervation he had once refused to set foot on. White home-steaders were clamoring for new lands throughout Indian Territory, and the Comanches and Kiowas had three million acres. The government wanted the tribes to sell off most of their land so that it could be opened to white settlement.

By now, there were only about twelve hundred Comanches left. Many of them opposed the government's plan. Quanah twice traveled to Washington to plead that Congress keep the reservation intact. When he realized that his cause was hope-less and that the reservation would be broken up, he changed his tactics and tried to get the best deal possible.

As a reservation chief, Quanah had learned to move easily through the white man's world. He lived in a fine house and entertained his guests around a big dining room table. On trips to Washington, he exchanged his Comanche buckskin for a suit and tie. But he never really abandoned the tribal traditions and beliefs that had nurtured him.

As he lay dying of pneumonia on February 22, 1911, the tribal medicine man stood by his bedside and flapped his hands over Quanah like the wings of an eagle—an eagle that would carry the chief's spirit up to the Great Spirit in the Comanche hereafter. The funeral procession—wagons and buggies of every description, along with a few automobiles and saddle horses—stretched for nearly two miles along the dusty road to the reservation cemetery. Dressed in the full ceremonial regalia of a Comanche chief, Quanah was buried beside his mother, Cynthia Ann, and his sister, Prairie Flower.

71

Quanah stands beside his wife To-ner-cy on the Comanche Reservation. As was the custom among the Comanches, Quanah had several wives. All of his twenty-five children were encouraged to learn the white man's ways.

Washakie

WASHAKIE

You must not fight the whites.
I not only advise against it,
I forbid it!

Every summer, the Shoshonis rode down from their mountain camps, carrying beaver pelts to the great fur trappers' rendezvous in the Wyoming wilderness. Thousands of Indians from many tribes showed up at this boisterous, month-long fur market. They mingled with white fur trappers, famous mountain men like Jim Bridger and Jedediah Smith. And they bartered with white traders who had journeyed all the way from St. Louis, exchanging their beaver pelts for muskets and gunpowder, for tools, cloth, tobacco, and ornaments.

A Catholic missionary, Father Pierre Jean de Smet, visited the rendezvous of 1840. He watched as the Shoshonis greeted the white traders with a grand parade:

"Three hundred of their warriors came up in good order and at full gallop into the midst of our camp. They were hideously painted, armed with war clubs and covered all over with feathers, pearls, wolves' tails, teeth and claws of animals, and outlandish ornaments.... Those who had wounds received in war, and those who had killed the enemies of their tribe, displayed their scars ostentatiously and waved the scalps they had taken on the ends of poles. After riding a few times around the camp, uttering at intervals shouts of joy, they dismounted and all came to shake hands with the whites in sign of friendship."

The Shoshonis had extended the hand of friendship to the whites as far back as 1805, when the explorers Lewis and Clark first arrived in their remote mountain homeland. They provided pack horses, food supplies, and Indian guides to help the explorers find their way through the mountains. Later, the Shoshonis befriended the trappers and traders who followed on the heels of Lewis and Clark. White traders who had Shoshoni wives were known as "squaw men." By the 1840s, friendship with the whites had become a tradition among the Shoshoni people.

Washakie had grown up in close contact with the whites. He was born in Montana's Bitterroot Valley about the time that Lewis and Clark passed through the region. His parents named him Pina Quanah, or Smell of Sugar. He was still a small child when his father was killed in a raid by Blackfoot warriors. The boy fled with his mother, two brothers, and two sisters. They found refuge with his mother's people, the Lemhi band of the Eastern Shoshonis, the group that Lewis and Clark had encountered.

One summer, young Pina Quanah herded ponies for a white fur-trapping party. When the trapping season ended, the Americans gave him an old musket. He showed it off to his friends, who had nothing more than bows and arrows. "After that," he later recalled, "all the young men of my tribe followed me, because I could shoot farther than they."

Pina Quanah gave up his childhood name after he killed

A Shoshoni camp in the foothills of the
Wind River Mountains, Wyoming, in 1870.

his first buffalo. He skinned the buffalo's head, removed the
hair, puckered the skin up, and tied it around a hollow stick
so that he could blow it up like a balloon. Then he put some
stones into it. When the skin dried, the stones rattled inside.
Later he carried his noisemaker into battle, shaking it violently
to frighten the enemies' horses. From then on he was known
as Washakie, or Rawhide Rattle.

His enemies had another name for him. They called him
Scar Face or Two Scar Chief, because he carried deep scars
from a Blackfoot arrow that had pierced his left cheek.

He proved his courage in many battles with the Blackfeet

75

and Crows. According to a favorite story of the Shoshonis, Washakie and two other warriors trailed a party of Blackfoot raiders all the way from the Green River in Wyoming to the Missouri River in Montana—a distance of six hundred miles. They returned home with the horses the Blackfeet had stolen and with most of the raiders' scalps.

Years later, as an old man, Washakie looked back at his youthful exploits with some regret. "As a young man I delighted in war," he said. "When my tribe was at peace, I would wander off sometimes in search of an enemy. I am ashamed to speak of those years, for I killed a great many Indians."

He was still a young man when he established a camp on the Green River and became leader of his own band. Around 1844 after the principal chief of the Eastern Shoshonis had died, Washakie took over as chief. Recognized as a great warrior, he also was admired as an orator, as a singer who accompanied his songs with a gourd rattle, and as an artisan who made fine bows and arrows from elk horns and cherry wood.

During these years, great changes were taking place in the Shoshonis' homeland. Most of the streams in the region had been overtrapped, and beavers were getting scarce. The white fur trappers and traders were moving on to new hunting grounds in the Pacific Northwest. Meanwhile, white emigrants bound for California and Oregon were traveling in growing numbers over the Oregon Trail, which passed directly through the territory of the Shoshonis and a number of other tribes.

Many of these tribes regarded the busy overland highway as a threat to their hunting grounds. The emigrants had to be constantly on guard against ambushes and raids by resentful Sioux, Cheyenne, and Arapaho warriors. Once they reached the country of the Shoshonis, however, the travelers could relax. The Shoshonis were known to be friendly. Was-

The covered wagons of emigrants bound for the Pacific move westward along the Oregon Trail in this sketch by W. H. Jackson. By 1869, when the first transcontinental railroad was completed, more than 350,000 emigrants had passed over the trail, depleting the timber, grass, and game of the Shoshonis and many other tribes.

hakie had forbidden his warriors to harm the whites who passed through their homeland. Shoshoni tribesmen often helped the emigrants ford rivers and round up their straying cattle.

Washakie had good reasons for staying on friendly terms with the whites. As far back as anyone could remember, the Shoshonis had been threatened and harassed by hostile tribes. Crow and Blackfoot warriors had pressed down from the North. The mighty Platte River Federation—the Teton Sioux with their Cheyenne and Arapaho allies—had attacked from the East. Outnumbered by these enemy tribes, the Shoshonis had been driven from the buffalo plains of Wyoming and Colorado and forced back into the Rockies, which became their stronghold.

As white trappers and traders arrived in their country, the Shoshonis came to depend on them not only for trade goods,

but also for firearms to be used against their enemies. Washakie knew that the whites could be powerful allies. He knew also that his people were not strong enough to survive a conflict with the whites.

He was determined to keep the peace, even though the Oregon Trail had already caused his people hardship and suffering. "This country was once covered with buffalo, elk, deer, and antelope, and we had plenty to eat," he told some Mormon emigrants. "But now, since the white man has made a road across our land, and has killed off our game, we are hungry, and there is nothing for us to eat."

Some emigrants were beginning to settle on Shoshoni lands. Once, in a fit of anger, Washakie lectured a group of white settlers who were operating a ferry service on the Green River. "This is my country and my people's country," he told them. "My father lived here and drank water from this river. My mother gathered wood on this land. The buffalo and elk came here to drink water and eat grass, but now they have been killed or driven out of our land.

"All the grass has been eaten off by the white man's horses and cattle. The timber has been burned. And now, when our young men have been hunting, and are tired and hungry, they come to the white man's camp and are ordered to get out. They are slapped, or kicked, and called 'damned Injuns.'

"Sometimes they have been so abused that they have threatened to kill all the white men they meet in our land. But I have always been a friend to the white man, and I have told my people never to moisten our land with his blood. To this day the white man cannot show in all our country where the Shoshonis have killed one of his people, though we can point to many abuses we have patiently suffered from him."

In 1859 the whites opened the Lander Road, which branched

off from the Oregon Trail and cut across both the Shoshonis' and the Bannocks' hunting grounds. When Washakie met Frederick Lander, the engineer who had blazed the trail, he told him he would not try to fight this new invasion of his country. He realized that his people could not conquer the whites or drive them away. He had always warned his young men that they could never win a war with the United States.

Despite his warnings, some warriors were talking openly of going on the warpath. They were angered by the growing traffic on the Lander Road, scaring off still more buffalo and game. "I am not only your chief," Washakie told them, "but an old man [he was in his fifties] and your father [their leader]. It therefore becomes my duty to advise you. I know how hard it is for youth to listen to the voice of age. The old blood creeps with the snail, but the young blood leaps with the torrent. Once I was young, my sons, and thought as you do now. Then my people were strong and my voice was ever for war. . . . You must not fight the whites. I not only advise against it, I forbid it!"

Many of the young men would not listen. They began to slip away from Washakie's village on the Green River to join the rebellious bands led by Bear Hunter, a militant Shoshoni chief, and Pashego, a chief of the Bannock tribe. In 1862 the rebels finally did go on the warpath, raiding white settlements near the Utah-Idaho border and ambushing wagon trains on the Oregon Trail. The army retaliated swiftly and in force. Cavalry troops attacked the rebels' camp in Idaho, killing over two hundred Indians, including Bear Hunter, and taking many prisoners. By the summer of 1863, the uprising was over.

Washakie had refused to take any part in the fighting. Afterward, he helped negotiate a peace settlement. Then he looked to the future. For years he had been asking that a

Washakie (front row, center) poses in a photographer's studio with other tribal leaders. Dick Washakie, his son, sits on his right.

reservation be set aside for his people in the Wind River region of Wyoming. Other Indian chiefs had fought the government's efforts to put their people on reservations, but Washakie had different ideas. With the coming of the whites, he argued, the Indians could no longer roam freely as hunters and warriors. The buffalo and other game were disappearing. He believed that the best path for his people to follow was to settle down and take up farming.

The Shoshonis' present home in the Green River Valley offered poor farming land. White settlements were beginning to crowd in on the area, and it was in the path of a planned railroad line. Washakie told government officials that if his people could move north to the fertile Wind River Valley, they would learn to grow crops and raise cattle.

His wish for a settled homeland was granted in 1868 by the Treaty of Fort Bridger, which established a three-million-acre reservation for the Shoshonis. In return, they gave up their claims to their remaining lands in Wyoming and Utah, and they promised to remain at peace with their white neighbors. Before agreeing to the treaty, Washakie went over it word by word with the help of two interpreters. One of them tried to explain the meaning of "latitude" and "longitude," which determined the boundaries of the new reservation. Washakie listened respectfully. He said that he hoped to learn more about latitude and longitude someday, but for the present, he wanted the boundaries of his reservation explained to him in terms of rivers and mountains.

He signed the treaty on July 4, 1868. By touching pen to paper, he promised to give up his ancestral way of life and become a tiller of the soil. Yet Washakie was jubilant. He had secured for his people the choicest part of their homeland, far to the north of the white settlements. "I am laughing because I am happy," he said at the signing, "because my heart is good."

He did not laugh long, for enemy tribes kept the Shoshonis from moving to their new home. There were still plenty of buffalo left in the Wind River country. At one time, the Shoshonis had fought the Crows for possession of these hunting grounds. They had since made peace with the Crows, but now Sioux, Cheyenne, and Arapaho raiders were harassing Shoshoni hunting camps along the Wind River.

Washakie wanted to move north, but he feared that his

outnumbered warriors would be hard-pressed to defend the region from their enemies. He demanded military protection. In 1869 the army established Camp Brown in the heart of the new Wind River Reservation. It wasn't until 1872, however, that the Shoshonis felt secure enough to settle there.

Despite the troops stationed at Camp Brown, the raids continued. "My reservation has been invaded many times by my enemy, the Sioux," Washakie complained. He had seen some of his finest warriors fall in battles with the Sioux. And he had a long-standing personal score to settle. During a battle a few years earlier, Washakie had seen his oldest son killed and scalped by Sioux warriors.

In 1876 he had a chance to get even with his enemies. Warfare had broken out in the Sioux country to the east. Sitting Bull, Crazy Horse, and other defiant chiefs had refused to settle on a reservation set aside for them in South Dakota. Army troops commanded by General George Crook had been ordered to catch the rebels and subdue them.

Crook needed Indian scouts to serve as his army's guerrilla arm. Eager to settle accounts with the Sioux, Washakie mustered a group of Shoshoni warriors to take part in Crook's campaign. The Shoshonis were joined by a contingent of Crows. In the past, the two tribes had often battled each other. Now they were allies. They were willing to fight shoulder to shoulder to assist the U.S. Army against their common enemy, the Sioux.

By now, Washakie was about seventy years old. Each morning he rode to a hilltop to scan the country through powerful field glasses. Then he reported his observations to General Crook. Later that day he drilled his mounted warriors while he carried the banner of the tribe—a standard of eagle feathers attached to a twelve-foot lance. One of Crook's officers

General George Crook recruited Shoshoni and Crow scouts to aid in his campaign against the Sioux.

described the scene:

"At a signal from Washakie, the column turned . . . and proceeded slowly for about 50 yards. Washakie was trying to explain something to me, but the noise of the ponies' hoofs and my ignorance of his language kept me from understanding what the old gentleman was driving at. I learned afterwards that he was assuring me that I was now to see a drill such as the Shoshonis alone could execute.

"He waved his hands. The line spread out. . . . Then the ponies broke into a frantic rush for camp, riding over sagebrush, rocks, stumps, bunches of grass, buffalo skulls—it mattered not the least when they went over it—the warriors all the while squealing, yelling, chanting their war songs, or howling like coyotes. . . . In the center of the line rode old Washakie, holding the eagle standard in front of him. It was an exciting and exhilarating race, and the force preserved an excellent alignment."

Shoshoni and Crow warriors played a key role in General Crook's campaign. They fought Crazy Horse and his forces at the Battle of the Rosebud in June 1876, turning back several Sioux charges that threatened to overrun the American position. They helped defeat the Cheyenne chief, Dull Knife, in the Big Horn Mountains in November 1878. And they provided the scouts that tracked Sitting Bull's movements as the army kept him on the run. By the spring of 1879, most of the fighting had ended. Crazy Horse had surrendered. Sitting Bull had fled to Canada.

In honor of Washakie's services to the United States, the

Rabbit Tail, a Shoshoni scout who fought with the U.S. Army. Note his bracelets, his ornamented vest, and his brass-studded mirror.

army changed the name of Camp Brown on the Wind River Reservation to Fort Washakie. President Grant sent the Shoshoni chief a gift, a handsome saddle with elaborate silver trimming. It was presented at a formal ceremony held on the fort's parade ground. During the speeches and band music, Washakie stood silently with his arms folded, but he appeared to be deeply moved. When the time came for him to speak, he hesitated, at a loss for words. After a long pause, he made his most famous statement: "Do a kindness to a white man, he feels it in his head and his tongue speaks. Do a kindness to an Indian, he feels it in his heart. The heart has no tongue."

Washakie was proud of the honor the United States had bestowed upon him, and pleased with President Grant's gift, but he wasn't pleased with the government's policies during the next few years. Officials in Washington wanted to break up the alliance of tribes that had fought together during the recent war. They decided to place the Sioux, the Northern Cheyennes, and the Northern Arapahos on widely separated reservations. Despite Washakie's objections, the Arapahos were moved to the Shoshoni reservation at Wind River. Since they were destitute and starving after years of war, Washakie agreed that they could remain on Shoshoni lands temporarily.

"These people have been enemies of the Shoshonis since before the birth of the oldest man," he said. "If you leave them here there will be trouble. But it is plain they can go no farther now.... Let them stay until the grass comes again. But when the grass comes again, take them off my reservation! I want my words written down on paper with the white man's ink. I want you all to sign as witnesses to what I have said. And I want a copy of that paper. I have spoken."

As it turned out, the Arapahos would remain permanently on the Wind River Reservation, where they live today.

Washakie with his grand-
daughter. The front of her
dress is covered with
elk's teeth.

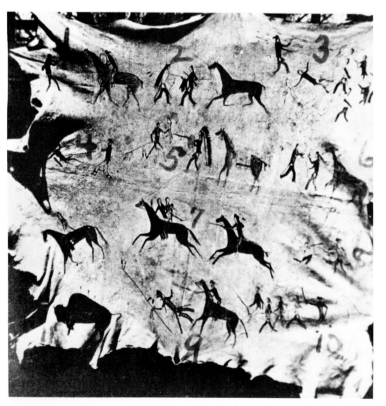

Scenes from Washakie's long life are
recorded in this elk-hide painting.

Meanwhile, whites were beginning to trespass on the reservation. White hunters were killing off large numbers of deer and antelope, and the few buffalo that still remained. White rustlers managed to spirit away most of the beef cattle the Shoshonis were raising to replace the buffalo. White gold miners had already taken over the southern part of the reservation. The government had paid the Shoshonis $25,000 to give up that land. The Indians had used the money to start the beef herds that were stolen by the rustlers.

"We have suffered many wrongs at the hands of the whites," Washakie told Governor John Hoyt of Wyoming Territory. "The white man, who possesses this vast country from sea to sea, who roams over it at will and lives where he likes, cannot know how cramped we feel in this little spot. You know as well as we that every foot of what you proudly call America, not very long ago belonged to the red man. The Great Spirit gave it to us. There was room enough for all his many tribes, and all were happy in their freedom. . . .

"And so, at last, our fathers were steadily driven out, or killed. We, their sons, sorry remnants of tribes once mighty, are cornered in little spots of the earth, all ours by right—cornered like guilty prisoners, and watched by men with guns who are more than anxious to kill us off."

He reminded Governor Hoyt that the United States had promised to keep both whites and other Indian tribes off Shoshoni lands. "But the government has not kept its word," he said. "The white man kills our game, captures our furs, and sometimes feeds his herds upon our meadows. And your great and mighty government does not protect us in our rights. . . . I say again, the government does not keep its word!"

As Washakie approached his eightieth birthday, his thoughts turned increasingly to the past. The walls of his cabin beside

Washakie wearing the silver peace medal
sent to him by President Andrew Johnson

the Little Wind River were covered with pictures he had painted himself on elk skins, showing scenes of his hunts, his buffalo chases, his triumphs as a great warrior. He had chosen to lead his people down the white man's road, and as he looked back, it seemed, perhaps, that he had no other choice. The Shoshonis had never been powerful. Their lands had been invaded by an endless stream of foreigners bringing with them a new civilization. Washakie had avoided much of the bloodshed that had plagued other tribes in the West. Many of those tribes had been scattered against their will to desolate reservations picked by the government, while he had secured for his own people the most fertile and beautiful part of their homeland. Even so, he longed for the old days when buffalo herds filled the plains and warriors rode out to hunt them.

Still vigorous, he would get on his horse and ride for miles across the Wind River country, a proud old man with a cascade of silvery hair. Sometimes he rode up into his beloved Wind River Mountains, the home of Tamapah, the Sun-Father. Washakie believed that from the heights of those mountains, he could see the land he would occupy after death. He could see it in the distant mists, its sparkling streams alive with fish, its green meadows abounding with deer and elk. There were horses in that land that never grew tired, new and comfortable lodges for all, and meat so plentiful that his people would never know hunger again.

As he passed his ninetieth birthday, his eyes and his memory began to fail, and the leadership of the Shoshonis passed on to younger men. Shortly before Washakie died on February 20, 1900, he sent a message to an old friend, Bishop Ethelbert Talbot of the Episcopal Church. He was too weak to speak, so he said in sign language: "Tell the good friend who has gone east that Washakie has found the right trail."

Chief Joseph

JOSEPH

From where the sun now stands,
I will fight no more forever.

Before the old chief died, he sent for Joseph, his son. "I saw that he was dying," Joseph recalled. "I took his hand in mine. He said, 'My son, my body is returning to my mother earth and my spirit is going very soon to see the Great Spirit Chief. When I am gone, think of your country. You are now the chief of these people. They look to you to guide them.

"'Always remember that your father never sold his country. You must stop your ears whenever you are asked to sign a treaty selling your home. A few years more and white men will be all around you. They have their eyes on this land. My son, never forget my dying words. This country holds your father's body. Never sell the bones of your mother and father.'

"I pressed my father's hand and told him I would protect his grave with my life.... I buried him in that beautiful valley of the winding waters. I love that land more than all the rest of the world."

At the age of thirty-one, Joseph took his father's place as chief of the Wallowa Valley band of the Nez Perce tribe. French-

Buffalo-skin lodges at a Nez Perce encampment on the Yellowstone River. Outside the tipis, war shields are mounted on tripods.

speaking fur trappers had called them the *Nez Percé,* or "Pierced Nose," Indians, because some of them wore ornamental seashells in their noses. The tribespeople adopted the name, which they pronounced *nez purse*.

Like other tribes, they were divided into many small bands, each living in its own villages and following its own leaders. For centuries they had roamed the valleys, canyons, and plateaus of the Rockies, in the region where Oregon, Washington, and Idaho now meet. They caught fat salmon in mountain streams, hunted for deer, elk, and antelope, and gathered wild onions, carrots, and berries. Every summer they sent hunting parties across the Bitterroot Mountains to the buffalo ranges of Montana for meat and hides. And they raised horses and cattle—fast horses and many cattle.

They had lived in peace with the whites ever since their first contact with French trappers around 1750. When the explorers Lewis and Clark arrived in Nez Perce country in 1805, weary and starving after struggling through the rugged Bitterroots, the tribespeople welcomed them and fed them. Forty years later, when young Joseph was growing up, the Nez Perces could still boast that they had never killed a white man.

Joseph was born in 1840 in the Wallowa Valley—the Land

of the Winding Waters—in northeastern Oregon, birthplace of his father and his ancestors. He was given the tribal name Hin-mah-too-yah-lah-ket, Thunder Rolling in the Mountains. His father, Tu-eka-kas, was known to the local whites as Old Joseph, so they called the son Young Joseph. His younger brother was named Ollokot, or Frog. They looked so much alike as boys that people mistook them for twins, but they turned out to be very different.

Ollokot was a good-natured giant of a man, highly popular among the tribespeople. He became a daring hunter and warrior who won many tribal honors in skirmishes with the Blackfeet and other tribes. Joseph was more reserved, by nature a thinker rather than a fighter. Even when he was young, people came to him for advice. Although he was shorter than Ollokot, he still stood six feet two inches tall, and he weighed two hundred solid pounds.

While Joseph and Ollokot were growing up, white settlers were streaming into the region. In 1855 the Nez Perces agreed to cede a small part of their territory to the United States. The country was vast, and the Indians believed there was room enough for everyone. After that, however, it seemed that the settlers' appetite for more land could never be satisfied.

In 1863 when Joseph was twenty-three, the government persuaded several Nez Perce chiefs to give up most of the tribe's remaining land and settle on the Lapwai Reservation in Idaho. Two-thirds of the chiefs, including Joseph's father, refused to sign the treaty setting up the reservation. They called it the Thief Treaty, and they ignored it. They continued to live, as before, outside the boundaries of the new reservation.

By the time Joseph replaced his father as chief in 1871, white ranchers had started to trickle into the Wallowa Valley.

Old Joseph, or Tu-eka-kas, father of Young Joseph. Gustave Sohon sketched this likeness in 1855.

Joseph spoke bitterly of these settlers. "They stole a great many horses from us and we could not get them back because we were Indians," he complained. "The white men told lies for each other. They drove off a great many of our cattle. Some white men branded our young cattle so that they could claim them. We had no friends who would plead our cause before the [white] law councils."

The Superintendent of Indian Affairs for Oregon summoned Joseph to a council and told him that his people would have to move to the Lapwai Reservation, whether they wanted to or not. "The white man has no right to come here and take our country," Joseph replied. "This land has always belonged to my people.... We are contented and happy if the white man will leave us alone. The Lapwai Reservation is too small for so many people with all their livestock."

At first, officials in Washington sided with Joseph. The Bureau of Indian Affairs declared that the Wallowa Valley still belonged to Joseph's band, since they had never agreed to the treaty of 1863. The whites were ordered to leave, but they refused. Instead, they began to build roads and bridges in the valley, and they threatened to force the Indians out. As more whites moved in, the government reversed its decision. In 1875, President Grant issued a proclamation officially opening the Wallowa Valley to white homesteaders.

Joseph tried to avoid trouble by moving to another part of the valley, away from the growing white settlements. "If we ever owned the land we own it still," he insisted, "for we never sold it." By now, the situation was getting ugly. Two ranchers had shot and killed an Indian youth after accusing him of stealing their horses. Joseph appealed to his people to remain calm, but the settlers feared an uprising. They demanded military protection.

Matters came to a head in May 1877 when Brigadier General Oliver Otis Howard was ordered to send his troops into the

General Oliver Otis Howard, the army's one-armed "praying general," pursued the Nez Perces from Idaho across the Rockies to Montana. Known as a humanitarian, Howard often spoke out on behalf of Indian rights.

valley. Howard was a Civil War hero who had lost his right arm during a cavalry charge. A man of deep religious convictions, he had a strong sense of justice and compassion. It was his personal belief that Joseph had every right to stay in the Wallowa Valley, and he said so in a report to Washington. "I think it a great mistake to take from Joseph and his band of Nez Perce Indians that valley," Howard had reported. But as an army officer, it was his duty to carry out orders.

Howard met with Joseph and the other nontreaty chiefs and told them: "You know that the government has set aside a reservation, and the Indians must go on it. I stand here for the President, and there is no spirit good or bad that will hinder me. My orders are plain and will be executed. I hoped that the Indians had good sense enough to make me their friend, and not their enemy."

Howard gave the chiefs thirty days to collect their belongings and move to the reservation. The chiefs protested. Thirty days didn't allow them enough time to round up their cattle and horses, pack their tipis and equipment, and move their people north. Yet none of the chiefs was willing to fight. Their outnumbered warriors would be no match for the howitzers and Gatling guns of Howard's troops.

"Many of our young men wanted to fight rather than be driven like dogs from the land where they were born," said Joseph. "I urged my people to be quiet and not begin a war."

And so Joseph led his people out of their homeland. They gathered their possessions and as much of their livestock as they could and traveled north to an ancient tribal meeting place in Rocky Canyon, near Tolo Lake. There they joined the nontreaty bands led by chiefs White Bird, Looking Glass, and Too-hool-hool-zote. The Lapwai Reservation was still a day's ride farther north.

JOSEPH

By now, most of the tribespeople had resigned themselves to the move. But some of the young men were still angry, and as they talked and brooded, they accused their chiefs of being cowards. On the morning of June 13 three warriors from White Bird's band slipped away from Rocky Canyon and rode south to seek revenge. The father of one youth had been shot by a rancher two years earlier in a dispute over some missing horses. Another youth had been whipped by the whites. The young men returned to the country they had just left. By nightfall, they had killed four settlers known to them as Indian haters. Later they were joined by about twenty other young warriors bent on revenge. The Indians continued their raids for two more days, rampaging through the countryside and killing fourteen or fifteen more whites.

During these raids, Joseph and Ollokot were away from the Rocky Canyon encampment, butchering beef on the other side of the Salmon River. When they returned and learned what had happened, the camp was in turmoil. Some people had already fled in panic. Joseph realized that war could not be avoided. The soldiers would be coming after them. He agreed with the other chiefs to pull out of Rocky Canyon and meet at the bottom of White Bird Canyon, sixteen miles to the south, where they would be protected from a surprise attack.

"I was deeply grieved," Joseph said later. "I would have given my own life if I could have undone the killing of white men by my people. I know that our young men did a great wrong, but I ask, 'Who was to blame?'"

Joseph had always thought of himself as a diplomat. He had never fought a battle until the morning of June 17, 1877.

Just before dawn that morning, a coyote's howl echoed through White Bird Canyon—the signal of Nez Perce scouts

97

that soldiers were approaching. As the soldiers emerged from a ravine and rode into the canyon, six mounted Indians were waiting under a white flag. A warrior shouted, "What do you people want?" The soldiers halted. Then one of them raised his rifle and fired two shots at the Indian truce team. Nez Perce sharpshooters returned the fire, and the first battle of the war was on.

About seventy warriors were hidden among the rocks and ridges on either side of the canyon. Within minutes, a dozen soldiers had been shot out of their saddles. Indians were advancing on horseback and on foot. Shots rang out from concealed Indian positions. The confused troopers broke ranks and began to retreat in panic. "The Indians were prepared for us and anticipated our arrival," one of the soldiers said later. "As soon as we got into the canyon, they had us flanked on all sides and we were completely routed."

Thirty-three soldiers had been killed. Only two Indians had been wounded. The Battle of White Bird Canyon entered the military record as one of the army's worst defeats at the hands of western Indians.

The Nez Perce War was to last through the summer and fall of 1877. General William Tecumseh Sherman would call the struggle "one of the most extraordinary Indian wars of which there is any record." Pursued at one time or another by ten separate army commands, the Indians would cover some seventeen hundred miles during a period of seventeen weeks. They would fight thirteen battles and skirmishes. In nearly every case, they either defeated the army troops or fought them to a standstill.

The Indians' skill in avoiding capture and their courage in battle won the sympathy and admiration of people all over the country. In every battle, the Indians were outnumbered.

These sketches of the Nez Perce campaign appeared in a western journal called *The Illustrated Wasp* on September 1, 1877.

They never had more than two hundred fifty able-bodied warriors to confront the combined military and volunteer forces that totaled about two thousand men. In addition to the warriors, there were some four hundred fifty Nez Perce women, children, and old people, along with their herds of cattle and some two thousand horses, all trying to escape from the troops and find a safe refuge.

The Nez Perce leaders included several chiefs besides Joseph. During the fighting they would meet in council and plan their strategy together. By tradition, none of the chiefs held absolute power. But as the army's campaign continued, it was Joseph who emerged as the symbol of Nez Perce resistance. His

99

Nez Perce warriors on parade years after the war. In all
their battles, the Nez Perces could claim with honesty that
they never tortured prisoners or scalped the dead.

opponents came to regard him as a military genius—"the Indian Napoleon," as the newspapers called him. With no military experience to guide him, he learned how to fight on the
battlefield. "The Great Spirit," he explained, "puts into the
heart and head of man how to defend himself."

After the army's defeat at White Bird Canyon, reinforcements were called in from as far away as Atlanta, Georgia.
Meanwhile, the Nez Perce bands were fighting their way east
toward the Bitterroot Mountains. Their plan was to cross the
mountain range and seek safety on the buffalo plains of Montana.

As they entered the Bitterroots, they started up the steep,
rocky Lolo Trail. General Howard followed with his troops.
Nez Perce scouts were watching the general's every move. The

Indians paced themselves to stay two days ahead of Howard. They began to call him "General Day-After-Tomorrow."

At higher elevations, the Lolo Trail was muddy and slippery. It rained almost every day, and there was frost at night, even in July. As the trail spiraled up into the mountains it became a narrow, windblown shelf, twisting around cliffs, clogged with boulders, blocked by fallen trees. Climbing the trail in single file were Nez Perce mothers with babies on their backs, small children who were just learning to walk, feeble old people, and exuberant boys daring and chasing each other in the most dangerous places. Older boys prodded the cattle along and led the horses. Anyone who lost balance and slipped would fall two thousand feet into the gorge below.

They made their way over Lolo Pass and started down the other side of the mountains. As they approached the Bitterroot Valley, they found the trail blocked by a crude log fort, built a few days earlier by army troops dispatched from Missoula, Montana. It was manned by thirty-five soldiers and two hundred civilian volunteers who had rushed up from the valley. The Indians sent word to Captain Charles Rawn, commander of the fort, that they wanted to talk.

On July 27 Joseph, White Bird, and Looking Glass rode up to the fort for a parley with Rawn. The chiefs asked to continue on their way without a fight. In return, they promised to move peacefully through the Bitterroot Valley, respecting the settlers and paying with gold dust and currency for any supplies they needed. Rawn refused. He would not let the Indians pass unless they agreed to surrender their weapons and horses. The chiefs said only that they would confer with their people, and the meeting broke up without agreement.

Rawn's volunteers did not want to provoke trouble and risk an attack against their settlements. Most of them accepted the

Looking Glass was one of the chiefs who led the Nez Perces across the Rockies. He fought bravely through the long retreat, only to be killed by a chance bullet in the closing moments of the war.

Indians' pledge to keep the peace. They quickly pulled out of the fort and went back to their families in the valley.

Early the next morning, Rawn and his remaining troopers heard singing high above their heads. Looking up, they saw the Nez Perces with their horses and cattle filing along a narrow ledge at the top of a steep canyon wall, where it seemed not even a goat could pass. The Indians had found another trail that bypassed the fort and led safely down into the valley beyond. Rawn didn't have enough men left to stop them. The embarrassed captain withdrew to Missoula, and his fort became known as Fort Fizzle.

The Nez Perces kept their promise, moving peacefully through the valley. When the settlers saw that the Indians meant them no harm, they relaxed. Shopkeepers sold provisions to the Nez Perces as they traveled south, and ranchers traded livestock with them. For the moment, they had left

General Howard and the war on the other side of the Bitter-root Mountains.

On August 8 the Nez Perces pitched camp on the banks of Beaver Creek in Montana's Big Hole Valley. It was a perfect resting place. The creek teemed with trout, their ponies grazed in grassy meadows, and the men rode up into the hills to hunt for antelope. General Howard was now several days behind them. The Montana settlers had seemed friendly. The Nez Perce chiefs believed they were out of danger, and that night the Indians slept soundly in their tipis.

They were unaware that soldiers had been watching them from distant treetops. A large force of cavalrymen and volunteers under Colonel John Gibbon had been sent from Helena, Montana, to intercept the Nez Perces. Gibbon's men

Colonel John Gibbon attacked a sleeping Nez Perce camp in Montana's Big Hole Valley on the morning of August 9. The Indians had no warning. All who took part in the struggle described it as one of the most bitterly fought battles in the annals of warfare.

attacked at dawn, while the Indians were fast asleep. His soldiers charged through the encampment, and in the wild confusion, men, women, and children were shot or clubbed down as they ran from their tipis. Some of the tribe's best warriors lost their lives trying to protect their families that morning. Joseph himself was seen racing through the camp, clutching his infant daughter in his arms.

The battle raged all day as the Indians rallied, drove the troopers back, and held them at bay on a low hill. Nez Perce sharpshooters concentrated their fire on the officers, killing or wounding half of them by midafternoon. Joseph and White Bird, meanwhile, were in charge of leading the women, children, and wounded to safety. Perhaps thirty Indians had been killed during the soldiers' first charge, and as the Nez Perces returned to bury their dead, an awful wailing arose. The people mourned and wept with such feeling that battle-toughened soldiers in their hillside trenches listened and trembled. "Few of us," said Colonel Gibbon, "will soon forget the wail of mingled grief, rage, and horror which came from the camp four or five hundred yards from us when the Indians returned to it and recognized their slaughtered warriors, women, and children."

The next day, the Indians prepared to withdraw. Gradually their warriors broke off the engagement so that they could act as a rear guard for the fleeing families. They had fought the troops to a standstill, and now they managed to escape, but at great cost. The army reported that eighty-nine Indians had been killed in the battle. At least fifty of the dead were women and children. Nearly every family had suffered a loss. Gibbon had lost thirty-three men, including most of his officers. "It was a gallant struggle," he said later. "Who would have believed that those Indians would have rallied after such a surprise and made such a fight?"

Granville Stuart's sketch of the Big Hole battleground

The war continued for two more months. Always on the run, the Indians with their horses and cattle fled south through the Montana buffalo country. They turned east and zigzagged through Wyoming's newly established Yellowstone Park as twenty-one cavalry companies under three commanders converged on the park, trying to intercept them and head them off. Then the Nez Perces turned north, moving back into Montana, fighting a running battle with cavalry troops that had caught up with them.

At one time, they had hoped to find a safe refuge on the Montana buffalo plains, but as they fled north they were harassed by Indian scouts working for the army. Their old allies, the Crows, fearing the army's power, refused to help them. Convinced that the plains country was unsafe, they decided

105

Nelson Miles as a brigadier general. Miles caught up with the Nez Perces in the foothills of the Bear Paw Mountains, trapping them when they were just forty miles from Canada and freedom. After the war, Miles championed the cause of Joseph and his people, urging that they be allowed to return to the Pacific Northwest.

to flee across the border into Canada, where Sitting Bull's rebellious Sioux had gone into exile earlier that year.

By now, the Nez Perces were weary. Many of them were wounded or sick. General Howard's army had fallen several days behind, so the Indians slowed their pace and finally stopped to rest at Snake Creek, in the foothills of the Bear Paw Mountains, only forty miles from Canada and freedom. They did not know that a new army commanded by Colonel Nelson Miles was advancing toward them from the east.

Miles' forces attacked on the morning of September 30 taking the Nez Perces by surprise. "We had no knowledge of Colonel Miles' army until a short time before he made a charge on us, cutting our camp in two and capturing nearly all our horses," Joseph recalled. "About seventy men, myself among them, were cut off. I thought of my wife and children, who were now surrounded by soldiers, and I resolved to go to them or die. With a prayer in my mouth to the Great Spirit Chief who rules above, I dashed unarmed through the line of soldiers. It seemed to me that there were guns on every side, before and behind me. My clothes were cut to pieces and my horse was wounded, but I was not hurt. As I reached the door of my lodge, my wife handed me my rifle, saying, 'Here's your gun. Fight!'"

In the first rush of confused fighting, both sides suffered heavy casualties. Joseph's brother, Ollokot, was killed that day, along with Chief Too-hool-hool-zote. By nightfall, the Nez Perces had driven the soldiers back from their camp. Indian men, women, and children began to dig frantically into the earth with butcher knives, frying pans, and their bare hands, building a network of trenches and dugouts. Snow had been falling since late afternoon, and now a rising wind whipped up a blizzard. The Indians crouched and shivered in their dugouts. In the hills above them, the soldiers held their positions and waited.

The Battle of the Bear Paws lasted for five days under a driving snow as the army brought in a twelve-pound cannon to bombard the Indians. A Nez Perce warrior named Yellow Wolf, Joseph's nephew, described the battle scene: "Bullets from everywhere. A big gun throwing bursting shells. From rifle pits, warriors returned shot for shot. Wild and stormy, the cold wind was thick with snow....A young warrior, wounded, lay on a buffalo robe dying without complaint. Children crying with cold. No fire. There could be no light. Everywhere the crying, the death wail....All night we remained in those pits. The cold grew stronger. The wind was filled with snow. Only a little sleep. There might be a charge by the soldiers. The warriors watched by turns....I felt the coming end. All for which we had suffered lost!"

General Howard, who had been trailing the Nez Perces for weeks, finally reached the battlefield on October 4. The next day, messengers carrying a truce flag were sent to the Nez Perce camp with the army's surrender terms: Give up and you can return to the Northwest in peace. By now, five of the leading Nez Perce chiefs had been killed. It was up to Joseph to negotiate with General Howard and Colonel Miles.

"I could not bear to see my wounded men and women suffer any longer," Joseph said. "We had lost enough already. Colonel Miles had promised that we might return to our country with what stock we had left. I thought we could start again. I believed Colonel Miles or I never would have surrendered."

At 4:00 P.M. on October 5 Joseph rode out of his camp, accompanied by five warriors who walked beside him. Over his shoulders he wore a gray woollen shawl pierced by bullet holes. General Howard and Colonel Miles were waiting at the top of a hill, flanked by junior officers and an interpreter. Swinging off his horse, Joseph handed his rifle to Miles. Then he turned to the army interpreter:

"Tell General Howard I know what is in his heart. What he told me before, I have in my heart. I am tired of fighting. Our chiefs are killed. Looking Glass is dead. Too-hool-hool-zote is dead. The old men are all dead. It is the young men who say 'Yes' or 'No.' He who led the young men [Ollokot] is dead. It is cold and we have no blankets. The little children are freezing to death. My people, some of them, have run away to the hills, and have no blankets, no food. No one knows where they are—perhaps freezing to death. I want to have time to look for my children and see how many of them I can find. Maybe I shall find them among the dead. Hear me, my chiefs! I am tired. My heart is sick and sad. From where the sun now stands, I will fight no more forever."

Colonel Miles had assured Joseph that his people would be

The Surrender of Chief Joseph. In Frederic Remington's painting, Joseph greets Colonel Nelson Miles while General Oliver Otis Howard looks on.

allowed to return to the Pacific Northwest and settle on the Lapwai Reservation. In Washington, officials did not see it that way, and Miles was overruled. The government decided that the surviving Nez Perces would never be permitted to return to their homeland. Instead, they would be sent into permanent exile in Indian Territory (Oklahoma). When Joseph heard this, his only comment was, "When will the white men learn to tell the truth?"

Miles urged the government to reverse its decision, but he was turned down. Ragged and half starved, the Nez Perces were transported by train to Fort Leavenworth, Kansas, under heavy guard. From there they were shuttled from one reservation to another, winding up on the Ponca Reservation in Indian Territory. Many of them died of malaria and other diseases. "We ought not to be forced into a country not fitted by climate to our health, a place where we cannot live—where the country will not let us live," said Joseph.

Early in 1879 Joseph traveled to Washington to plead his case with high-ranking government officials. "I want the white people to understand my people," he told them. "Some of you think an Indian is like a wild animal. This is a great mistake. I will tell you about our people, and then you can judge whether an Indian is a man or not...."

"I have carried a heavy load on my back ever since I was a boy. I learned then that we were but few, while the white men were many, and that we could not hold our own with them. We were like deer. They were like grizzly bears. We had a small country. Their country was large. We were content to let things remain as the Great Spirit Chief made them. They were not, and would change the rivers and mountains if they did not suit them...."

"As for the war, I blame my young men and I blame the white men. I blame General Howard for not giving my people time to get their livestock away from Wallowa. I do not acknowledge that he had the right to order me to leave Wallowa at any time. I deny that either my father or myself ever sold that land. It is still our land. It may never again be our home, but my father sleeps there, and I love it as I love my mother. I left there hoping to avoid bloodshed...."

"If the white man wants to live in peace with the Indian, he can live in peace. There need be no trouble. Treat all men alike. Give them all the same law. Give them all an even chance

Eleven years after the war, Joseph visits peaceably with an old adversary, General John Gibbon.

to live and grow. All men were made by the Great Spirit Chief. They are all brothers. The earth is the mother of all people, and all people should have equal rights upon it....

"Whenever the white man treats the Indian as they treat each other, then we shall have no more wars. We shall be all alike—brothers of one father and one mother, with one sky above us and one country around us, and one government for all."

By now, thousands of people throughout the nation had rallied to Joseph's cause. Colonel Miles (now a General) and other influential whites continued their appeals to the government. Finally, in the spring of 1885, the Nez Perces were

allowed to leave the Ponca Reservation and return to the Northwest. Of the four hundred seventeen people who had surrendered with Joseph, only two hundred sixty eight were left. When they reached Idaho, they were separated into two groups. Some were sent under military escort to the Lapwai Reservation. Joseph and the others were assigned to the Colville Reservation in the state of Washington.

Joseph still hoped to return to the Wallowa Valley. "I want to go back there to live," he told a friend. "My father and mother are buried there. If the government would only give me a small piece of land for my people in the Wallowa Valley, with a teacher, that is all I would ask."

In 1900 he visited the valley for the first time since the war. More than twenty years had passed. Fences and irrigation ditches crisscrossed the landscape, and towns had sprung up along the winding Wallowa River. Yet the valley wasn't really that different. People lived in houses instead of tipis, but they still raised livestock and horses, as the Indians had done. Joseph visited his father's grave. And he attended a public meeting where he was told that he and his people would never be sold land anywhere in the valley.

He ended his days on the Colville Reservation, choosing to live in a tipi rather than the house provided for him by the government. On September 21, 1904, while sitting by his tipi fire, he collapsed and died at the age of sixty-four. The reservation doctor reported the cause of death as "a broken heart."

At the funeral ceremony, his nephew Yellow Wolf said: "Joseph is dead, but his words are not dead. His words will live forever."

Joseph in 1903, a year before his death. "I have no grievance against any of the white people," he said.

Sitting Bull

SITTING BULL

Indians! There are no Indians left but me!

As a boy, he was called Hunk-es-ni, or Slow, because he was so careful and deliberate in everything he did. Some people thought he was a bit slow in the head, too. But he soon outgrew his childhood name. He killed his first buffalo when he was ten and won his first battle honor when he was fourteen.

His father had given him a slender coup stick made of carved bone, and Slow waited for a chance to use it. The greatest honor a Sioux warrior could earn was to strike an enemy with his hand, his weapon, or his special coup stick. This was called "counting coup," from the French word for "blow." The warrior who counted coup most often and with the greatest daring was the hero of the battle.

Slow's chance came when a war party left his village to chase after some trespassing Crows, old enemies of the Sioux. The boy painted his pony red and himself yellow, slipped away, and followed the older men. When they caught up with the Crows, Slow charged forward on his pony. He overtook a Crow warrior, struck him with his coup stick, then galloped safely out of range before the surprised Crow could fire an arrow.

The next evening around the campfire, covered all over with the black paint of victory, Slow acted out the story of his first coup. According to custom, the older warriors, each in turn, testified that the story was true, saying, "That is the way it happened," or, "I was there, and I saw him strike the enemy."

Slow's father, a warrior named Sitting Bull, swelled with pride as he listened to the men talk about his son's exploit. The time had come to recognize the boy's courage, and the father cried out that he would bestow his own name on his brave son. From then on, the boy was known as Ta-tan-ka Yo-tan-ka, or Sitting Bull, while his father adopted a new name, Jumping Bull.

Young Sitting Bull was born in 1831 near the Grand River, in present-day South Dakota. His people were Hunkpapas, one of seven tribes that made up the mighty Teton Sioux nation. *Dakota* comes from a Sioux word meaning "allies" or "friends," and the Dakota plains were the shared hunting grounds of all seven Teton Sioux tribes.

While Sitting Bull was growing up, the first wagon trains were rolling westward along the Oregon Trail. But that was well to the south of the Hunkpapas. White soldiers and settlers had not yet invaded their part of the country.

Sitting Bull was still a youth when he earned membership in the Strong Hearts, an elite warriors' society. He suffered his first battle wound during a Strong Heart raid against the Crows. He had singled out a Crow warrior wearing a red shirt trimmed with ermine—the insignia of a chief. Both men were armed with guns. Sitting Bull dropped to one knee, thrust out his buffalo-hide shield, and took aim, but the Crow got off the first shot. The bullet ripped through the shield and tore

Winter encampment of
Sitting Bull's band

into Sitting Bull's left foot. Then he fired. As his enemy fell,
he limped forward and plunged his knife into the Crow chief's
heart. The gunshot wound caused him to walk with a limp
for the rest of his life.

In time, Sitting Bull would claim personal victory over more
than sixty enemy soldiers. His reputation as a warrior grew,
and during the 1860s he was named chief of the Hunkpapas.

By then, his people were beginning to feel the pressure of
the white man's advance on the western plains. Not far to the
east, homesteaders were streaming onto the Dakota prairie.
To the west, army troops guarded work on the new Bozeman
Trail, which ran from the Oregon Trail to the booming gold-
mining camps around Virginia City, in Montana Territory.

Sitting Bull feared an invasion by the whites as much as any invasion by enemy tribes, and he watched their movements with growing resentment.

In 1866 army troops marched deep into Hunkpapa territory to build Fort Buford at the junction of the Yellowstone and Missouri rivers, in present-day North Dakota. Sitting Bull regarded Fort Buford as a threat. He retaliated by leading his Strong Hearts in a series of raids against the fort and the surrounding countryside, terrorizing soldiers and civilians as far as two hundred miles up and down the river. That same year, Chief Red Cloud of the Oglala Sioux was attacking army forts and travelers along the Bozeman Trail. By 1868 the government was ready to negotiate a peace settlement.

A peace council was held at Fort Laramie. The government agreed to abandon the Bozeman Trail. It offered to set aside a big chunk of Dakota Territory as a permanent reservation for the Sioux and their allies. To the west of the new reservation, the Powder River country in Wyoming would be preserved forever as an Indian hunting ground. In the words of the agreement: "No white person or persons shall be permitted to settle upon or occupy any portion of the [Powder River country]; or without consent of the Indians . . . to pass through the same."

Along with several other Sioux and Cheyenne chiefs, Sitting Bull refused to attend the peace talks. Father Pierre Jean de Smet, the veteran Catholic missionary, traveled up the Missouri River to visit Sitting Bull's camp. He urged the chief to accept the Fort Laramie Treaty in the interests of peace. Sitting Bull pointed out that while the treaty seemed generous, it would actually take away much of the territory claimed by the Sioux. "The Great Spirit gave us this land, and we are at home here," he told Father de Smet. "I will not have my people

An army wagon train moves through the Black Hills in 1874. The discovery of gold in the Hills set off a stampede of miners and led to the Sioux War of 1876.

robbed.... I want everyone to know that I do not propose to sell any part of my country."

Many other chiefs, including Red Cloud, signed the treaty and agreed to settle on the Great Sioux Reservation. Sitting Bull never did sign. With the other nontreaty chiefs, he continued to pitch his camps outside the reservation, in the Powder River country. He intended to live in the old way by hunting the buffalo, not by accepting handouts from Washington. He taunted the reservation Indians by saying, "You are fools to make yourselves slaves to a piece of bacon fat, some hardtack, and a little sugar and coffee."

119

For a while, the nontreaty bands were able to avoid the whites. But they soon realized that the Fort Laramie Treaty would not hold back the advancing frontier. The Northern Pacific Railroad was planning to lay its tracks through the heart of the Powder River country. Meanwhile, prospectors had started to explore the Black Hills inside the Great Sioux Reservation, a region forbidden to whites.

In the eyes of the Sioux, the Black Hills were sacred, a place where spirits dwelt. They called the hills *Paha Sapa,* the center of the world. Young warriors went there to seek visions and speak to the Great Spirit. Now gold seekers were scouring the center of the world. By 1875 hundreds of them were camped illegally in the Black Hills.

Army troops made an effort to chase the gold miners away, but nothing could keep them out for long. As more miners streamed into the area, the government offered to buy the Black Hills from the Indians. Washington sent a commission to the Sioux reservation to negotiate a sale. As the commissioners arrived, they were greeted by three hundred Sioux warriors who galloped up to them firing their guns into the air and singing:

> The Black Hills is my land and I love it
> And whoever interferes
> Will hear this gun.

For nearly two weeks, the commissioners tried to persuade Sioux leaders to give up the Black Hills. But no chief was willing to take responsibility for selling sacred land. When the commissioners returned empty-handed to Washington, the government decided on a showdown. If the Black Hills could not be purchased, then the Powder River country—which was not part of the Sioux reservation—could be taken away from the Indians.

SITTING BULL

In November 1875 the Commissioner of Indian Affairs announced that all Indians living in the Powder River country were a threat to the reservation system. Sitting Bull and the other nontreaty chiefs were ordered to report at once to the Great Sioux Reservation. When the chiefs ignored the order, army troops were dispatched to round up the hostile bands and bring them in by force.

As the troops took to the field, thousands of warriors were gathering to fight them. Sitting Bull had sent messengers to every Sioux and Cheyenne band for hundreds of miles around, on the reservation and off, summoning them to a great war council on Rosebud Creek in southern Montana. "We are an island of Indians in a lake of whites," Sitting Bull declared. "We must stand together or they will rub us out separately. These soldiers have come shooting. They want war. All right, we'll give it to them!"

By June 1876 an enormous rebel camp had formed on the Rosebud, with hundreds of newcomers arriving each week. Perhaps fifteen thousand Indians had gathered here, among them some four to five thousand able-bodied warriors. Indian tipis stretched for three miles along the banks of Rosebud Creek and extended a half-mile inland.

Red Cloud of the Oglala Sioux—who only eight years earlier had won his war with the U.S. Army—wasn't at Rosebud Creek. He had elected to sit this war out, warning his followers to stay on the reservation with him. Many of his young men, including one of his sons, rejected his advice. They joined the rebels led by Crazy Horse, who replaced Red Cloud as the leading war chief of the Oglalas.

That month, as they prepared for war, the Sioux held their sacred sun dance ceremony. Sitting Bull was as much a spiritual leader as a war chief, and he sought divine guidance by dancing himself in the ancient religious ritual. He was now

Sioux Sun Dance. Practiced in various forms by more than twenty plains tribes, the sun-dance ceremony was the most important religious ritual of the year. This Jules Tavernier painting depicts a Sioux sun dance in 1874.

forty-five years old, a sturdy man almost six feet tall with a big head and a big nose. His pale brown skin was scarred by smallpox, his manner was still slow and deliberate, and he still limped on his lame left foot.

His hands and feet were stained red and his shoulders streaked with blue stripes, representing the sky. A brother warrior knelt beside him. With a needle-pointed awl, he cut fifty small pieces of flesh from each of Sitting Bull's arms, from wrist to shoulder. As his blood trickled and clotted, Sitting Bull began the slow, rhythmic dance dictated by custom,

122

bobbing up and down on his toes as he stared at the rim of the sun and prayed. He danced continuously for a day and a night and well into the next day, without food or water, until he fell exhausted to the ground and received the vision he had prayed for. He saw army soldiers falling from the sky like grasshoppers, with their heads bowed and their hats falling off. They were falling right into the Sioux camp. When Sitting Bull awoke, he announced that the Sioux would win a great victory.

While he was dancing and praying, three columns of army troops were advancing toward the Indian encampment from the south, the east, and the west. The advance column under General George Crook was spotted by Indian scouts on June 16. The next morning, Sioux and Cheyenne warriors led by Crazy Horse took Crook by surprise as he camped beside Rosebud Creek.

The Battle of the Rosebud was a standoff. Crook was saved by his Crow and Shoshoni scouts, who threw back several Sioux attacks that threatened to overwhelm the army troopers. Late that afternoon, Crazy Horse withdrew, leaving Crook in possession of the battlefield. But he had stopped the general's advance and inflicted heavy casualties. Crook's forces would be out of action for a month.

After the battle, the Sioux and Cheyennes moved to a new campsite on the west bank of the Little Bighorn River. A week later, Sitting Bull saw his vision of a great victory come true.

On the afternoon of June 25, 1876 the Sioux-Cheyenne camp was attacked by the Seventh Cavalry Regiment, commanded by Lieutenant Colonel George Armstrong Custer, the famous Indian fighter. "I could whip all the Indians on the continent with the Seventh Cavalry," Custer had boasted. He was so confident, so anxious to taste victory that day, that he allowed himself to act recklessly. Custer didn't realize how big the Indian encampment was. He ordered his men into battle without waiting for reinforcements from other army units that were on their way to join him. And he made a fatal tactical error by dividing his forces against an enemy that greatly outnumbered him.

Five companies of cavalrymen, led by Custer himself, were to ford the Little Bighorn and charge into the northern end of the Indian camp. Three other companies, led by Major Marcus Reno, would create a diversion by attacking the southern end of the camp. But Custer's plan collapsed at the start. Reno never had a chance. His troops were stopped within minutes and driven back by a thousand shouting warriors. Half of his 115 men were dead, wounded, or missing before he could retreat to a hilltop and dig in.

Custer didn't even make it across the Little Bighorn River. His five companies of cavalrymen were surrounded and overwhelmed on a low hill overlooking the river. A Sioux warrior who was there said that the Indians charged toward Custer's troops "like a hurricane...like bees swarming out of a hive."

Sitting Bull left it to Crazy Horse and the other war chiefs to engage the enemy. He sat on his war horse, armed with a Winchester carbine and a .45 revolver, watching the battle and planning strategy from a distance. Custer and his troopers were shrouded by clouds of gunsmoke and dust as they tried to save themselves. When the dust settled, all of them lay dead on the hillside, stripped of their weapons and clothing. Many of the soldiers were scalped, but not Custer. His body was found with a bullet wound in the head and one in the chest.

Major Reno's surviving troopers remained pinned down on their hilltop to the south, where they managed to fight off Indian attacks all night long. The next day, Sioux scouts re-

124

George Armstrong Custer, the celebrated "boy general" of the Civil War. After the war, as a lieutenant colonel, Custer gained a glowing reputation as an Indian fighter. He fought his last battle on June 25, 1876, at the Little Bighorn.

Custer's Last Stand. This impression of the famous
battle appeared in the *New York Graphic and Illustrated
Evening News* on July 19, 1876.

ported that army reinforcements were approaching. Sitting
Bull and the other chiefs decided to call off the battle, break
camp, and head for the Bighorn Mountains. Along the way,
the Indians split up into separate bands, each taking a different direction as they vanished into the mountains.

"All my warriors were brave and knew no fear," Sitting Bull
said later. "The soldiers who were killed were brave men too,
but they had no chance to fight or run away. They were surrounded too closely by our many warriors. . . . We did not go
out of our own country to kill them. They came to kill us and
got killed themselves."

The Battle of the Little Bighorn became known as "Custer's

Meeting Between the Lines. Frederic Remington
portrays Sitting Bull and Colonel Nelson Miles,
flanked by warriors and troopers, as they meet
in the middle of a field.

Last Stand." It was the worst defeat ever suffered by the U.S. Army at the hands of Indians, much worse than the Fetterman Massacre ten years earlier. Custer had led perhaps 220 men to their death—no one knows the exact number. The nation was shocked, and the government vowed to break the Indians' resistance. Reinforcements poured into the Sioux country. From then on, the Indians found themselves on the defensive.

Sitting Bull and his followers were pursued across Montana by Colonel Nelson Miles. Three times that fall, Sitting Bull agreed to meet with the colonel. At one meeting, the two men sat on horseback in the middle of a clearing, watched by lines of warriors at one end and cavalrymen at the other. Miles tried to persuade the Sioux chief to surrender his arms and

report peacefully to the reservation. Sitting Bull insisted that his people should be able to live freely in the Black Hills and the Powder River country, as promised by the Treaty of Fort Laramie. He told Miles: "The Great Spirit made me an Indian, but not a reservation Indian, and I don't intend to become one!"

The meetings settled nothing, and the fighting continued. As winter approached, the Indians were running low on food and ammunition. Several Sioux and Cheyenne chiefs decided to give up. Tired of being chased, they surrendered their arms to Miles and led their people off to the reservation. Miles continued to hunt down the bands that were still holding out. His fur-clad troopers attacked Indian camps even when temperatures fell far below zero.

In February 1877 Sitting Bull and his people fled across the border to seek refuge in Canada. Crazy Horse held out a while longer. He surrendered in May, leading about fifteen hundred of his followers into the reservation as they defiantly sang war songs and displayed their weapons. Later that year, soldiers on the reservation tried to arrest Crazy Horse as a suspected troublemaker. When he resisted, he was stabbed in the stomach with a bayonet. He died a few hours later, at the age of thirty-five.

By now, the Indians had lost everything they had fought for. Pressured by the government, the reservation chiefs had agreed to surrender both the Black Hills and the Powder River country. About a third of the land guaranteed to the tribes by the treaty of 1868 had been taken away. Except for Sitting Bull and his followers in Canada, all the Sioux and Cheyennes were now confined to their diminished reservation.

Sitting Bull stayed in Canada for four years. The government there tolerated his presence but refused to give his people food or other assistance. They were hungry most of the time, since the buffalo and other game had just about disappeared from that part of the country. Gradually, small groups of ragged, homesick exiles began to drift back to the United States, surrendering to army troops at the border. What little clothing they had was dropping off their bodies. By the summer of 1881 Sitting Bull's band had dwindled to fewer than two hundred people.

On July 19 the chief himself crossed the border. He surrendered at Fort Buford, where his triumphant warriors had once terrorized soldiers and civilians alike. He gave his Winchester rifle to his eight-year-old son, Crowfoot, and motioned for the boy to hand it over to Major David Brotherton. Defiant

Crow Foot, Sitting Bull's son. He handed his father's Winchester rifle to Major David Brotherton at Fort Buford in 1881. Sitting Bull later insisted that the boy had surrendered, not he.

even in defeat, he said: "The land I have under my feet is mine again. I never sold it. I never gave it to anybody."

For two years, Sitting Bull was held at Fort Randall as a prisoner of war. Released in 1883, he was allowed to return to his birthplace on the Grand River, near the Standing Rock Agency of the Sioux reservation. He was now a celebrity, probably the most famous Indian in the country, known to everyone as the man who had defeated Custer. People wrote to him from all over the world, Indian leaders called on him to seek his advice, and newspaper reporters came to interview him.

One reporter found him as self-confident as ever: "There was an inexpressible dignity in the strong face of the old chieftain, as he stood there on the prairie, with one moccasined foot thrown lightly forward, while the weight of his sinewy body rested solidly on the other foot.... The red and yellow paint smeared on his cheeks, and the gaudy girdle of porcupine quills and beads seemed trivial and out of harmony with the eagle nose, straight, powerful mouth, and the general sense of reserved power, which expressed the born commander of men."

Everyone who visited the Sioux reservation wanted to meet Sitting Bull. Buffalo Bill Cody, the celebrated frontier scout and showman, called on him in 1885. He persuaded the Sioux chief to join his Wild West Show for a tour of the eastern United States and Canada. Billed as "The Slayer of Custer," Sitting Bull was a big attraction. Curious crowds lined up to see him and buy his autographed picture, which he sold for twenty-five cents. He gave most of the money to the beggar boys who waited outside the theaters and followed him everywhere. When the tour ended, Buffalo Bill presented the chief with a gift—a gray horse trained to sit down and raise a hoof at the sound of a gunshot.

130

Sitting Bull poses with Buffalo Bill during his tour with the Wild West Show in 1885.

When Cody asked Sitting Bull to travel to England with the Wild West Show in 1886, the chief turned him down. "It is bad for our cause for me to parade around like this," he said. "Besides, I am needed here. There is more talk of taking our lands."

The Sioux had already lost the Black Hills and the Powder River country. Now the government wanted them to sell off a large part of their reservation for settlement by white homesteaders. Sitting Bull opposed the surrender of more land at any price. At a Sioux council meeting, he proposed that they get a scale and sell the earth at so much per pound. He became so troublesome, so effective at obstructing negotiations, that reservation officials tried to keep him from speaking at public meetings on the issue.

Other Sioux leaders were afraid the land would be taken away from them whether they sold it or not, so they finally agreed to sell some eleven million acres. The Great Sioux Reservation was split up into five smaller reservations, and each Sioux family received 320 acres of private land. A newspaperman asked Sitting Bull how the Indians felt about giving up more of their land. "Indians!" he shouted. "There are no Indians left but me!"

He knew that the Indians were losing more than land. Signs of change were everywhere. Instead of hunting wild game, people now traveled long distances to their reservation agencies to draw government rations. Children came home from school with their hair cut short and challenged the tribal wisdom of their parents. Reservation officials banned ceremonies and rituals that had been handed down for generations. The sun dance was forbidden, and the old peace pipe religion was discouraged. To enforce these rules, the government established a special police force made up of Indians, to replace

Ration day on the reservation

the old warrior societies. The policemen wore blue uniforms
and badges—the other Indians called them Metal Breasts.
They were well paid. And they received extra rations and
special privileges.

Meanwhile, living conditions on the reservations were growing steadily worse. A succession of droughts and blizzards
during the 1880s caused crop failures and hardship. Congress

decided to economize by cutting the Indians' beef ration in half. Epidemics of measles, influenza, and whooping cough swept through the reservation villages, killing many under-nourished children.

By 1890 thousands of Indians on reservations throughout the West had turned to a new religion that promised to deliver them from misery and despair. The new faith had been founded in Nevada by a Paiute mystic named Wovoka. He preached that the Indians could overcome their hardships and bring back the old world as it had existed before the white people arrived. To do this they must renounce war and violence, pray to the Great Spirit, and perform religious rites that included a special dance, accompanied by a chant. Wovoka claimed that this slow, shuffling dance had been revealed to him in a vision. The dancers could bring on a trance that would allow them to glimpse the future: millions of buffalo would return to the plains. The whites would vanish. Indians from the past would rise from the dead, and those now alive would live forever.

As they looked back, many Indians believed they had lived in a paradise before the whites came. By performing Wovoka's shuffling dance and chanting his magical chant, they could bring back that paradise. The new religion spread rapidly from tribe to tribe across the West. The whites called it the ghost dance religion.

Sitting Bull was himself a mystic and a respected religious leader. He had always lived in close communion with the spirit world, but he had his doubts about Wovoka's new faith. "It is impossible for a dead man to return and live again," he said. Even so, he did not discourage the believers who began to gather in front of his cabin every day to dance, pray, and seek visions.

Ghost dancers. Many dancers fell into trances and saw visions of better days to come.

As the ghost dance movement spread, white authorities began to worry. They feared that trouble was brewing, and they suspected that Sitting Bull would be the man to lead any mass uprising. "Indians are dancing in the snow and are wild and crazy," reported a reservation official. "We need protection and we need it now."

Some eight thousand army reinforcements were rushed to the reservations. Orders went out to arrest Sitting Bull and confine him to a military compound until he was no longer a threat to peace.

Just before daybreak on December 15, 1890, a force of forty-three Indian policemen commanded by Lieutenant Henry Bull Head surrounded Sitting Bull's cabin. Bull Head and several others burst into the cabin. They shook Sitting Bull awake, ordered him to get dressed, and hustled him outside. About 150 of the chief's followers had gathered at the scene. As they started to protest, Sitting Bull stopped short and shouted, "I'm not going! Do with me what you like. I'm not going!"

The police tried to clear a path through the angry crowd. A shot rang out, hitting Lieutenant Bull Head in the side. As he fell, he turned and fired a shot that struck Sitting Bull. Then another policeman, Sergeant Red Tomahawk, who had been pushing Sitting Bull from behind, shot the chief in the head. Sitting Bull's trained horse, his gift from Buffalo Bill, was standing by the chief's cabin, saddled and waiting. As the first shots were fired, the horse sat down on cue and raised his hoof to shake hands.

By the time the shooting stopped, six policemen and eight of Sitting Bull's followers, including his seventeen-year-old son, Crowfoot, had been killed or fatally wounded. The remaining policemen took refuge inside the cabin until soldiers came to rescue them two hours later. Sitting Bull was not yet sixty when he died that morning.

The last major battle of the Indian wars took place two weeks after the killing of Sitting Bull. Frightened by the sudden appearance of so many army troops, hundreds of Indians had fled from their reservation agencies and were hiding out in the Dakota Badlands. Soldiers fanned out to find the runaway bands.

On December 28, 1890 troops of the Seventh Cavalry, Custer's old regiment, caught up with a Sioux band led by Chief Big Foot and brought them to an army camp at Wounded Knee Creek. There were 120 men in Big Foot's band and 230 women and children. The next morning, as soldiers tried to

Red Tomahawk (left) was one of forty-three Indian police sent to arrest Sitting Bull. When a crowd gathered and firing broke out, he shot Sitting Bull in the back of the head.

Big Foot's band at a ghost-dance ceremony in August 1890.
Four months after this photo was taken, some two hundred
members of the band lost their lives at Wounded Knee Creek
in the last major battle of the Indian wars.

disarm the Indians, a medicine man began to perform the
ghost dance and chant a holy song. One of the Indians pulled
a gun from his blanket and fired wildly. The soldiers replied
instantly, shooting back at point-blank range with their car-
bines and with four small cannons placed on a nearby hill.
Warriors rushed the soldiers and grappled with them, using
knives, war clubs, and pistols. Within a matter of minutes, the
fight was over. More than two hundred Sioux men, women,
and children had been shot down. Sixty-four soldiers lay dead
or wounded, many of them killed by their own bullets or flying
shrapnel. The sound of the firing had been heard clearly at
the Pine Ridge reservation agency, almost twenty miles away.

138

SITTING BULL

The Battle of Wounded Knee Creek, known to the Indians as the Wounded Knee Massacre, marked the end of the Indian wars in the American West. The Indians had lost the West, and a great deal more. Perhaps they found comfort in the words of Sitting Bull, who had said: "If a man loses anything and goes back and looks carefully for it, he will find it."

Soldiers on horseback plod through the snow as they return from the fight at Wounded Knee.

BIBLIOGRAPHY
INDEX
PHOTOGRAPHIC SOURCES

BIBLIOGRAPHY

Andrist, Ralph K. *The Long Death: The Last Days of the Plains Indians.* New York: Macmillan Publishing Company, 1964.

Beal, Merrill D. *"I Will Fight No More Forever": Chief Joseph and the Nez Perce War.* Seattle: University of Washington Press, 1963.

Brown, Dee. *Bury My Heart at Wounded Knee.* New York: Holt, Rinehart & Winston, 1970.

Capps, Benjamin. *The Great Chiefs.* New York: Time-Life Books, 1975.

Chalmers, Harvey. *The Last Stand of the Nez Perce: Destruction of a People.* New York: Twayne Publishers, 1962.

Commager, Henry Steele, with Marcus Cunliffe and Maldwyn A. Jones (eds.). *The West: An Illustrated History.* New York: Exeter Books, 1984.

Connell, Evan S. *Son of the Morning Star: Custer and the Little Bighorn.* San Francisco: North Point Press, 1984.

Custer, George A. *My Life on the Plains.* Lincoln: University of Nebraska Press, 1966.

Edmunds, R. David. *American Indian Leaders.* Lincoln: University of Nebraska Press, 1980.

Fehrenbach, T. R. *Comanches: The Destruction of a People.* New York: Alfred A. Knopf, 1974.

Gidley, M. *Kopet: A Documentary Narrative of Chief Joseph's Last Years.* Seattle: University of Washington Press, 1981.

———.*With One Sky above Us: Life on an American Indian Reservation at the Turn of the Century.* New York: Putnam, 1979.

Hassrick, Royal B. *The Sioux: The Life and Customs of a Warrior Society.* Norman: University of Oklahoma Press, 1967.

Hoebel, E. Adamson, and Wallace, Ernest. *The Comanches, Lords of the Southern Plains.* Norman: University of Oklahoma Press, 1964.

Hyde, George. *Red Cloud's Folk: A History of the Oglala Sioux Indians.* Norman: University of Oklahoma Press, 1975.

Jackson, Clyde L., and Jackson, Grace. *Quanah Parker: Last Chief of the Comanches.* New York: Exposition Press, 1963.

Josephy, Alvin M., Jr. *The Patriot Chiefs: A Chronicle of American Indian Resistance.* New York: Viking Press, 1961.

McCracken, Harold. *George Catlin and the Old Frontier.* New York: Dial Press, 1959.

Marrin, Albert. *War Clouds in the West: Indians and Cavalrymen, 1860–1890.* New York: Atheneum, 1984.

Mayhall, Mildred P. *The Kiowas.* Norman: University of Oklahoma Press, 1971.

Nye, Wilbur Sturtevant. *Bad Medicine and Good: Tales of the Kiowas.* Norman: University of Oklahoma Press, 1962.

Reynolds, Sidney O. "The Redskin Who Saved the White Man's Hide." *American Heritage,* February 1960.

Rister, Carl Coke. "Satanta, Orator of the Plains." *Southwest Review,* Autumn 1931.

Scott, Douglas D., and Connor, Melissa A. "Post-Mortem at Little Bighorn." *Natural History,* June 1986.

Trenholm, Virginia Cole, and Carley, Maurine. *The Shoshonis: Sentinels of the Rockies.* Norman: University of Oklahoma Press, 1964.

Utley, Robert M. *The Indian Frontier of the American West, 1846–1890.* Albuquerque: University of New Mexico Press, 1984.

Vestal, Stanley. *Sitting Bull: Champion of the Sioux.* Norman: University of Oklahoma Press, 1957.

INDEX

(Italicized numbers indicate pages with photos)

INDEX

INDEX

149

PHOTOGRAPHIC SOURCES

The prints and photographs in this book are from the following sources and are used with permission:

The Bancroft Library, University of California: page 99

The Texas Collection, Baylor University: pages 52, 56

Denver Public Library, Western History Collection: pages 77, 137

The Thomas Gilcrease Institute of American History and Art, Tulsa, Oklahoma: pages 31, 68

Kansas State Historical Society: page 47

Library of Congress: Frontispiece and pages 13, 21, 23, 25, 36, 40, 60, 109, 126, 127, 131

Montana Historical Society, Helena: page 105

National Archives: pages 2, 14, 16, 18, 19, 35, 45, 59, 61, 66, 83, 86, 88, 102, 103, 106, 119, 122, 125, 129, 133, 138, 139

Oregon Historical Society: page 95

Smithsonian Institution: pages 5, 8, 10, 26, 28, 34, 42, 43, 49, 55, 70, 75, 90, 92, 111, 112, 114, 117, 135

Western History Collections, University of Oklahoma Library: page 84

Special Collections, University of Washington Libraries: page 100

Archives-American Heritage Center, University of Wyoming: pages 72, 80

Washington State Historical Society: page 94

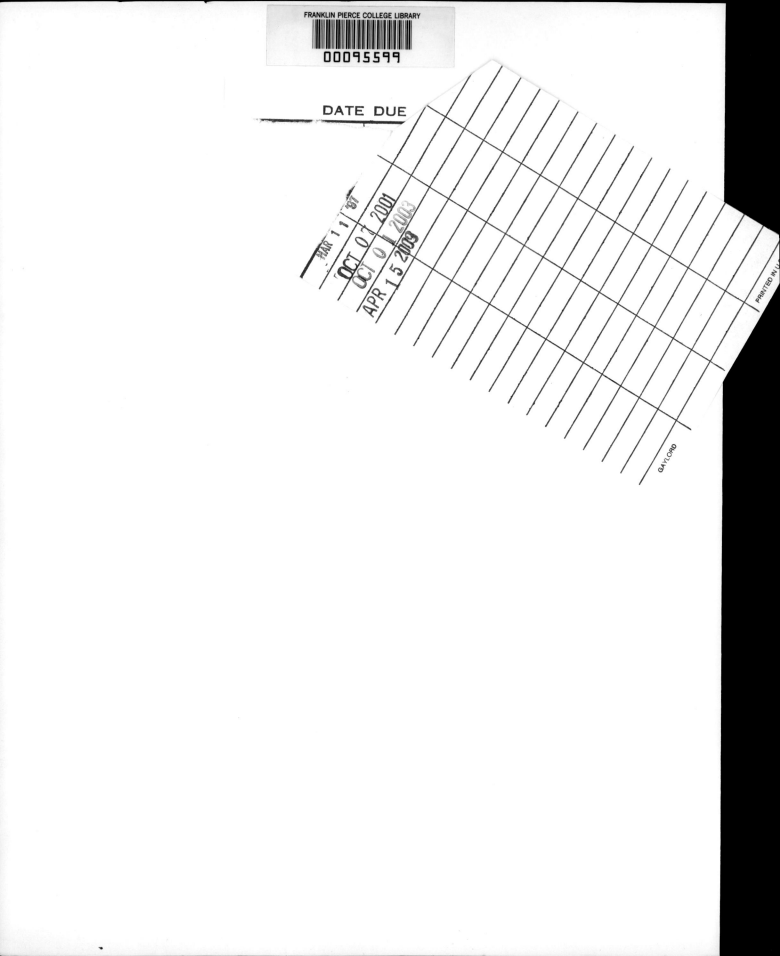